Storytelling
in the Digital Age

A Guide for Nonprofits

Julia Campbell

PRESS ™

Nonprofit Storytelling in the Digital Age

One of the **In the Trenches™** series

Published by
CharityChannel Press, an imprint of CharityChannel LLC
424 Church Street, Suite 2000
Nashville, TN 37219 USA

CharityChannel.com

ISBN: 978-1-938077-79-1

Library of Congress Control Number: 2017942480

13 12 11 10 9 8 7 6 5 4 3 2 1

Printed in the United States of America

This and most CharityChannel Press books are available at special quantity discounts for bulk purchases for sales promotions, premiums, fundraising, or educational use. For information, contact CharityChannel Press, 424 Church Street, Suite 2000, Nashville, TN 37219 USA. +1 949-589-5938.

Publisher's Acknowledgments

This book was produced by a team dedicated to excellence; please send your feedback to Editors@CharityChannel.com.

We first wish to acknowledge the tens of thousands of peers who call *CharityChannel.com* their online professional home. Your enthusiastic support for the **In the Trenches**™ series is the wind in our sails.

Members of the team who produced this book include:

Editors

Acquisitions: Amy Eisenstein

Manuscript Editing: Suzanne M. Gustafson

Copy Editing: Stephen Nill

Production

Layout: Stephen Nill

Design: Deborah Perdue

Administrative

CharityChannel LLC: Stephen Nill, CEO

Marketing and Public Relations: John Millen

About the Author

Julia Campbell, MPA, has a long history of helping nonprofits learn how to best use the latest marketing and fundraising tools. After ten years in the nonprofit sector as a development director and marketing coordinator, she founded J Campbell Social Marketing, a boutique digital marketing agency based in Wenham, Massachusetts.

Julia received her bachelor's degree in journalism and communications from Boston University, a master's degree in public administration from Old Dominion University, and a certificate in nonprofit management from Tidewater Community College.

A returned Peace Corps Volunteer (Senegal 2000-2002), mother of two, and lover of social causes, Julia helps her nonprofit clients connect with supporters by effectively harnessing the power and potential of online marketing and social media tools. Julia offers small-group coaching sessions, workshops, seminars, and online courses, and counts small, community-based nonprofits and large universities among her clients. Her blog has been named one of the Top 150 Nonprofit Blogs in the world.

Julia has been featured on Maximize Social Business, About.com, MarketWatch, Alltop, Salon, Social Media Today, *Forbes,* and Business 2 Community. Her latest thoughts on all things nonprofit can be found at her blog—*jcsocialmarketing.com/blog.* She would love to hear from you about your successes and challenges in digital storytelling! Please contact her at julia@jcsocialmarketing.com or find her on Twitter @JuliaCSocial.

Dedication

This book is dedicated to my husband, Evan, and my children, Isabelle and Colin—I love you!

Author's Acknowledgments

This book would not be possible without the unwavering support and backing I received from friends and family. I need to expressly thank my patient husband and kids for putting up with hours spent at the computer; my parents, stepparents, and in-laws for always offering to help out wherever needed; and my friends for their enthusiasm and confidence in me. Running a business, taking care of a family, and writing a book are no easy feat—I certainly could not have done it alone.

I want to sincerely thank Stephen C. Nill, CEO of CharityChannel Press, for believing in this book and the importance of this topic, and his help and guidance through every step of the process. I greatly appreciate Suzanne M. Gustafson's keen eye and detailed edits—thank you.

Recognition goes to nonprofit fundraising superstar Amy Eisenstein, ACFRE and CharityChannel Press author, who encouraged me to go for it and submit a book proposal.

I am grateful to all of my mentors and colleagues who motivate me to do this work and give me fantastic ideas and inspiration—John Haydon, Debra Askanase, Joanne Fritz, Heather Mansfield, Pamela Grow, Sandy Rees, Joe Waters, and Beth Kanter (just to name a few). I remember the moment I realized that I could actually do this work and make a living at it—it was entirely due to the encouragement and support that I received from this network of generous, kind, and brilliant people.

Last, but certainly not least, I want to acknowledge the hard work and dedication of nonprofit professionals everywhere. You are the tools and agents of change—not Facebook, not Twitter, not Instagram, not whatever social media channel will appear tomorrow. This sector employs the most resilient, creative, and committed people in the world, and I count my blessings every day that I get to help them with their important work.

Contents

Summary of Chapters

We Are All Storytellers. I will provide you with an explanation of the benefits of storytelling as a vital marketing and fundraising strategy for nonprofits. We will cover the definition of digital "storytelling," the fundamental building blocks of a story, and the reasons to use stories to connect with donors and supporters.

Culture Shift: Creating an Army of Storytellers. I explain how to dispel misconceptions about nonprofits' use of social media and how to build a storytelling culture at your organization. I will also explain how to create policies and procedures to involve and empower staff and volunteers to collect and tell stories on your nonprofit's behalf.

Creating a Storytelling Plan. We will go into the nuts and bolts of creating a storytelling plan with SMART (Specific, Measurable, Actionable, Realistic, and Time-based) goals and objectives for a digital storytelling campaign. I will also help you identify specific audiences for your messages and how to tailor your messages to each such target audience.

The Stories You Need to Tell. I will describe the six types of stories that nonprofits should be telling in their communications with supporters.

Places to Find Great Stories Your Donors Will Love. I will detail the multitude of places you can find great stories for your nonprofit and how to convince people to share their own stories. We'll also help you create a storytelling calendar to help track your stories and ideas.

Stories That Turn People from Passive to Active. We'll cover how to tell a story that compels people to take action. We'll discuss how to develop a narrative arc and hook for the story, the importance of focusing on people versus programs, and other storytelling tips.

Addressing Common Challenges in Storytelling and Social Media. We'll discuss common challenges that nonprofits face in telling their stories, such as confidentiality issues and reluctance on the part of staff and clients to share their experiences. I'll cover what to do if you don't have a so-called "sexy cause" and how to coach clients into becoming great storytellers. We'll also discuss working with a storytelling consultant in your storytelling efforts and creation of a social media policy for your organization.

Your Nonprofit Website and Mobile Strategy. We'll cover ways to integrate storytelling into your website—a nonprofit's most vital marketing asset. I'll explain the explosion in popularity and use of mobile technology and tools, and how nonprofits can adapt to this change in communication via specific changes or additions to their websites.

Storytelling Through Your Nonprofit Blog. We'll cover the basics of nonprofit blogging—why you need one and the best platforms to use; how to get more readers to your blog; how to find and create fresh content for your nonprofit blog; and the top ten tips for creating fantastic blog posts. We'll also discuss maintaining your nonprofit's blog once it's up and running.

Creating Great Nonprofit Emails That Inspire Action. We'll cover the best practices in nonprofit email marketing, how to build a powerful email list, and how to integrate email marketing efforts with your website and social media channels.

How to Use Social Media to Tell Your Story. I'll explain the
best practices for using social media to tell your nonprofit story,
including specific nonprofit storytelling examples from Facebook,
Twitter, and Instagram.

Visuals and Video—Spice up Your Storytelling. We'll dive into
creating visuals to augment your stories and where and how to best
use visuals online. I'll also provide tips for incorporating recorded and
live video in your storytelling efforts.

Measuring Results and Building on Successes. We'll explore some
easy ways to gauge the success of your storytelling campaign. I will
also show you how to extend the life of your stories and build on the
momentum you have created.

The storytelling calendar template will help you determine where and
when to collect and to tell stories. Use it to write down all upcoming
milestones, events, and happenings that are relevant to your organization
and your donors.

The social media content calendar template is a place to collect ideas for
social media posts on each channel. Use it to plan out your social media
posting schedule weeks or even months ahead of time.

The blog editorial calendar is a repository for blog topic ideas, draft titles,
deadlines, and other notes that will help keep your blog on schedule.

The measurement spreadsheet template is designed for the
collection of relevant metrics and data on your website traffic, social
media engagement, and email marketing effectiveness. Use this
spreadsheet for easy reporting and examination of trends in your
digital storytelling efforts.

Your Social Media "Superfans" need a place where they can readily
access visuals, videos, and facts about your organization to share with
their networks. This checklist provides a sample of what could be
included to make sharing your message easier and more streamlined.

Foreword

For years, a well-known breast cancer foundation in New York City has held an annual walkathon to create awareness and raise money to fight breast cancer.

And each year, its message was the same: breast cancer impacts a surprisingly large number of women—young and old. Its messaging included the powerful statistics that about one in eight women getting diagnosed with breast cancer during their lifetime, that almost fifty thousand women die each year from breast cancer, and that breast cancer is the second leading cause of cancer death in women (behind lung cancer).

Although these statistics clearly demonstrated the urgent need to fight breast cancer, the foundation's walkathon results remained flat year after year.

Then everything changed. One year, after seeing that the walkathon results were not increasing, the organization's leadership developed a new strategy that created a 33 percent surge in online fundraising! This new approach was so simple and so powerful that the executive director could not understand why organization leaders had not thought of it before.

Can you guess what this magical plan was? The organization started telling better stories. Its previous statistic- and data-focused messaging shifted to focus on a story of a grandmother who had breast cancer. In its emails to supporters and through its social media posts, the nonprofit told the story about this woman's life as a grandmother, her fears and hopes, and how, in the end, all she really wanted was to see her grandkids grow up.

When told from this heart-centered place, stories like these also include the donor. The donor feels involved, because such an emotional storytelling framework essentially wraps the donor into the narrative. And in this organization's case, the donor went from being simply a source of funding (like an ATM) to a hero in the story about people fighting breast cancer.

Nonprofits often have a very good grasp on what they do regarding the programs that they provide and the number of people (or animals, or landscapes, for example.) that they help every day. However, they are often hesitant to tell the emotional stories of these people—the beneficiaries of their great work—due to misconceptions about social media, assumptions about storytelling, and of course, a serious lack of time to do it all.

That's why *Storytelling in the Digital Age: A Guide for Nonprofits* is a vital must-read for even the smallest of nonprofits. It is a tactical, hands-on guide to collecting and telling great stories, even if your nonprofit has never done so before.

Part One of this book lays the foundations necessary to mobilize staff, volunteers, and other constituents and transform your nonprofit culture into one that embraces and encourages storytelling.

Part Two is a detailed guide to finding, writing, and sharing compelling stories, as well as addressing some very common storytelling challenges— some of which I am sure your nonprofit faces.

Part Three delves into details about the digital tools you need to use to share your stories with supporters. Whether you share stories on your website, through your email newsletter, on your blog, or via your social media platforms (or, ideally, all of the above!), this book will provide you with action items and tips for getting the most return on investment in your digital storytelling efforts.

Julia is a natural storyteller, and I've been a big fan from the beginning. And I love it when I get an opportunity to work with her, whether it's formulating strategy for a nonprofit or presenting a course together.

She's a pro, through and through, but her knowledge (and mastery) of storytelling shines. You will see it in every page in this book.

But it's not just that she's a great author. She lives and breathes storytelling. You'll notice if you follow her on Instagram. She shares pictures of pride events with her friends. She shares advocacy posts about women's rights and LGBTQ rights. And a year ago, she helped organize a fundraiser for a family whose child unexpectedly died.

Julia will tell you the story of stories. How stories were born, how they grew up in the age of social media and mobile devices, and how nonprofits can use them to build vibrant, engaged, and giving online communities of supporters.

John Haydon
Author, *Facebook Marketing for Dummies*
Speaker and Coach

Introduction

Digital storytelling. What first comes to mind when you hear this term? Joy? Terror? Confusion? Love it or hate it, I am willing to bet that you have heard this term being thrown around the Internet, at conferences, and in news reports. The concept of digital storytelling has received an overwhelming amount of press, publicity, and hype—and has nonprofits in a frenzy to keep up.

There is no doubt that storytelling works in getting a message across, and that digital marketing tools are being used successfully by nonprofits to raise awareness about causes and campaigns. The question remains: How can great stories and online tools be connected in a strategic way to help nonprofits better achieve their fundraising and marketing goals? Most importantly, how can busy staff members or volunteers at a stretched-thin organization manage to keep up with it all while not losing their minds (or sense of humor)?

While the thought of finding compelling stories, collecting them, and then mastering the digital landscape to showcase them may give you hives, I assure you that, in even the smallest nonprofit organizations, this can be done well. Storytelling without the Internet is like crackers without cheese, like coffee without cream. (Or tea, if you prefer.) – TASTELESS –

Storytelling is a perfect communication and fundraising strategy when you want to become more transparent and accessible to supporters. It is a compelling way in which to showcase your impact and engage your most passionate advocates, old and new. Websites, email, blogs, and social media are all dynamic online channels through which you can spread your stories far and wide. When used together, the possibilities are endless!

Brands and businesses are getting their stories out there—stories about their origins, their values, their customers, their successes. So why are most nonprofits so bad at digital storytelling? One reason is the tendency of nonprofits to feel uncomfortable talking about themselves. They don't want to be in the spotlight; they just want to put their heads down and do their jobs. They feel awkward asking for support, asking for attention, or patting themselves on the back.

There are also many challenges faced by nonprofits when using online forums to tell their stories. Issues of confidentiality, proprietary information, and intellectual property—not to mention the time to do it all—should all be front and center in our minds when opening the digital can of worms.

Storytelling in the Internet Era

Great storytelling is the best way to capture the attention, as well as the hearts and minds, of your supporters. Using modern digital tools like websites, email newsletters, and social networks are vital in the quest to get your stories in front of a critical mass of people.

Working together, the power of great stories and the reach of digital channels will inspire people to take a desired action (i.e., change a behavior, sign a petition, attend a rally, donate), and make it easy and desirable for your current supporters to share the story with their networks.

The goal of this book is to simplify the digital storytelling process and make it accessible to nonprofits that may not yet have explored these waters. This book will increase your confidence in storytelling, provide clarity about the online tools you need to use to share your stories, and give you inspiring ideas for your next fundraising and marketing campaign.

We will walk through a step-by-step plan to create a dynamic storytelling strategy first, and then we will provide best practices for promoting these stories using online tools like social media. We will also discuss the best ways to use all of the online communications channels at your disposal—your website, blog, email, and social media—to share and promote your stories.

The Value of Storytelling

When I served with the United States Peace Corps between 2000 and 2002, I learned firsthand the value of storytelling to communicate messages. I had arrived in Senegal, West Africa with a group of one hundred other volunteers, most of us just out of college and inspired to change the world. A group of us were trained as health educators and lived with Senegalese host families in remote rural villages with no electricity or running water. Our task: to identify, recruit, and train villagers to serve as health *relais*. The health *relais*, or volunteers, would receive formal education in malaria, HIV, and cholera prevention, as well as the importance of vaccinations and prenatal care. They would then take that information back to the villagers and spread the word.

The other Peace Corp volunteers and I spent hours preparing comprehensive health training for the *relais*. Since we were in rural Africa, many of the *relais* could not read, so we filled binders with visuals, comics, diagrams, and the like. We had all the bases covered. Or so we thought.

When our first official training day arrived, the health *relais* sat patiently and politely as we went through the statistical data, the to-do lists from the World Health Organization (WHO), and the best practices in preventative health care. We meticulously reviewed the materials in the binders before opening the floor to questions.

One woman tentatively raised her hand. She thanked us for our wonderful training and said that she had learned a lot of valuable information that she could take back to her village. Hesitating to criticize, she quietly asked: *But how will this make our friends and family members change their behavior?*

What we American volunteers failed to realize was that all of our carefully compiled, WHO-approved research would not mean the slightest thing to people in the villages. Statistics and research alone just don't compel people to take action and to change behaviors that have been going on for years.

We immediately revamped the training and spent the rest of the morning asking the *relais* for their ideas and input. How could we incorporate the cultural history and stories of the region? How could we use visuals to relay the information in a way that was interesting and would elicit emotion? How could we overcome the influence of harmful local traditions by using real-world examples? How could we best spread the word about this information to the maximum amount of people?

Our clinical training evolved into an invaluable brainstorming session on storytelling and using stories to convey important information about using malaria nets, washing vegetables, using clean water, and getting vaccinations. The realization that stories conveyed messages more completely than data and research helped the people in the village take better care for themselves and their communities.

Why Storytelling Is so Effective

Storytelling gets at the heart of how humans process information. When we hear stories, we immediately relate them back to an existing experience to determine how we feel about it. Humans are inherently narcissistic in this way. But this characteristic is precisely what makes storytelling so effective for marketing purposes.

The first modern storytelling campaign around a social cause was carried out in 1787 by the Society of Effecting the Abolition of the Slave Trade. The society compiled emotional stories of the conditions of the slave trade and shared them in graphics, at public events, and in print. It mixed facts and data with the horrific experiences of individual slaves to get its point across.

The invention of the printing press, the telegraph, the telephone, and eventually, the Internet made it easier and quicker than ever to share our thoughts, memories, and personal stories with others. The first "web log,"

Say It with Feeling

A study conducted by Root Cause and Fidelity Charitable found that when donors are looking for information about social causes and nonprofits, they tend to care most about "long-term benefits and impact." Only providing donors with hard data on your nonprofit outcomes is not nearly as compelling as demonstrating that impact with storytelling.

The hard truth about storytelling versus using data to connect with supporters is that people tend not to remember bullet points; they respond to emotion. And feelings, not analytical thinking, drive action and donations.

Dale Carnegie reportedly famously said, "When dealing with people, remember you are not dealing with creatures of logic, but with creatures of emotion, creatures bristling with prejudice and motivated by pride and vanity." Stories will help you express your mission to people who may know nothing about you or your cause initially. Statistics may shock and awe for a moment, but they will rarely get people to act. And getting people to take the desired action is the key because that is what nonprofit communication is all about!

 practical
tip

or "blog," was created by Justin Hall in January 1994. When Hall created his now-famous "Justin's Links from the Underground" blog (*links.net*), he wanted to "use the web to publish my personal notes on life." In the early 2000s, blogging took off as a way to share individual stories and experiences online to a wide audience, in real time. Now, human interest stories are shared widely across multiple platforms and channels, on social media, via email, on websites, in marketing materials, and in fundraising campaigns. Perhaps the most popular storytelling blog thus far, Humans of New York, collects stories and photos about real people on the streets of New York City. These stories often go viral on social media channels and have even spawned a bestselling book.

There is no doubt that online communication prioritizes stories and, even more so, a good story with a compelling photo. This is good news for nonprofits because organizations across the world are making a significant impact on the lives of others and they have inspiring stories to tell.

Today, charity: water, a nonprofit group, uses Instagram to tell the stories of families who have been given access to clean drinking water. The Denver Rescue Mission shares success stories from its clients on Facebook with accompanying photos. The St. Baldrick's Foundation uses its blog to showcase real-world stories from the children it has helped through funding cancer research. Share Our Strength uses its website to showcase true stories from its No Kid Hungry campaign. The examples (and the potential for storytelling using social media) are never-ending! (And are a good reference when starting your own nonprofit's storytelling campaign!)

Social media and digital tools have proven themselves to be very valuable in reaching constituents, supporters, and the worldwide community. According to research done by Waggener Edstrom, of social media users who support nonprofits online, 56 percent said that compelling storytelling is what motivated them to take action in the first place.

Let's Get Back to Basics

The *principles* of storytelling and the power it has on communication have not changed since the abolitionist movement, but the *landscape* in which to tell stories certainly has. Digital technologies have fundamentally changed the way people read and consume information. If your nonprofit is not embracing digital and social media tools to spread the word about your cause, your organization could be getting lost in the noise.

Like it or not, digital tools like social media have revolutionized and completely changed the way humans consume and share information as well as the ways we communicate with each other. Competing entities vie for your donors' attention on a moment-by-moment basis.

Your donors and constituents expect information shared with them to be interesting, unique, and compelling. They expect transparency, authenticity, and a bit of personality. They expect to get answers to their questions mere minutes after they ask them. They expect that there will be a real person on the other end of the computer and email address. They have been trained to expect 100 percent responsiveness and accessibility.

People want to receive information and stories that inspire and motivate— even to share with their own networks. That's where your nonprofit's stories

---

You're Never Too Old

According to research conducted by Heather Mansfield and reported on the website Nonprofit Tech for Good, nonprofits today need to be aware that they are dealing with five distinct generations of donors and supporters:

◆ Generation Z (Born 2001–Present)

◆ Millennials (Born 1980–2000)

◆ Generation X (Born 1965–1979)

◆ Baby Boomers (Born 1946 –1964)

◆ Silent Generation (Born 1925–1945)

You may think that your older donors are not online or using social networks. This is a myth! Pew Internet recently found that 72 percent of online adults between fifty and sixty-four years old are on Facebook and 62 percent of online adults aged sixty-five+ use the social network. LinkedIn is also a popular social network among older consumers, with 24 percent of online adults aged fifty to sixty-four and 20 percent of online adults aged sixty-five+ using LinkedIn. In fact, as a result of the increasing number of older adults using Facebook, its use increased 7 percentage points with online adults compared to the survey Pew Internet conducted just one year ago!

observation

come into the picture. In today's fast-paced, always-online world, we all must function like media companies—discovering and disseminating timely, relevant, and interesting information to our target audience. To be an effective nonprofit leader, you need to be able to tell your nonprofit's story, and you need to be able to tell it online.

With the overwhelming selection of online tools available to us, it can be easy to put the cart before the horse—to start with the tools (such as getting a Facebook page or creating a Twitter account) before we know what we are going to say and why. Nonprofit organizations need to get back to the basics of storytelling first and figure out the methods of dissemination second.

Stories are necessary to inspire your supporters to take action when they are online. Then, with a click of a mouse, they can share that action with their own personal networks. Putting a great story in a direct mail piece is certainly important, but if this is the only place the story lives, it is not easily shared and could die an unfortunate death after the mailing is forgotten. (Can you imagine your donors photocopying your appeal letter and mailing it out to their friends?)

Widespread Internet connectivity has made the process of sharing great stories and taking action such as donating money or joining a movement so much more simple and cost effective. This book will teach you how to take advantage of these new technologies while creating stories that your supporters will want to share and spread far and wide.

Embracing the digital world in which we live and using these powerful new tools is imperative, but it's not the first step. The principles of success in the digital space are the same whether you are a large nonprofit or a small one. It's not about how many tools you use. It's about how you use them.

No matter which tools are popular six months from now or ten years from now, the principles of connecting to and engaging with people through stories will remain the same.

Benefits of Going Digital

Eighty percent of nonprofits identify their website as their most important communication channel, according to the 2016 Nonprofit Communications Trends Report. This report also found that 71 percent of nonprofits surveyed are currently using social media, 59 percent will pay for Facebook advertising this year, and 31 percent plan to post to Facebook an average of once per day.

In addition to your nonprofit peers, Pew Internet reported that almost 80 percent of online Americans now use Facebook, with roughly three-quarters reporting that they visit the site daily. Your supporters, your constituents, and your nonprofit competitors are using these tools to find each other. How are you going to remain competitive if you don't?

Success online is about being of value to a group of people and igniting their passions. For nonprofits, this means being less focused on what your organization wants to say and more focused on what your stakeholders want to hear. It's about building a community of like-minded individuals you can count on and call on (after you have given them a good reason).

Engaging donors, raising awareness, and creating trust are all things that digital tools do well. It's never a waste of time to connect with others who are interested in what you do. Social media channels, in particular, are perfect avenues by which to spread your nonprofit's stories far and wide and to get instant feedback, validation, and confirmation of your important work.

The sheer amount of online content competing for supporter and donor attention forces nonprofit professionals to dig deep into this vital question: *Why should anyone care about us?* You know why you do what you do. You understand why people should donate, volunteer, and attend events. But can you convey this to a person not familiar with your nonprofit or your issue? You want to highlight to these as-yet nonsupporters the good work your nonprofit does to help the community and its clients.

Due to their always-on, up-to-the-minute nature, social media help provide a richer and more comprehensive picture of your nonprofit and its mission. How can you use your online real estate to make the world care about your mission? Can your story cut through the clutter and the noise on social media? And if not, what are you doing wrong, and how can you get noticed?

In the increasingly competitive landscape for donors' attention and support, getting people to notice and to hear your message can seem impossible. When used in conjunction with great stories, email communications, social media, and mobile tools will help you form deeper connections with your donors and supporters.

Storytelling Is Empowering

At its best, storytelling should be empowering for your organization and the community you serve. It is not exploitative or disingenuous. The process itself should be empowering and strengthening. Not intimidating and scary, but thrilling!

Combining storytelling with social media tools is one of the best ways to gain exposure for your cause, to connect with current stakeholders, and to recruit new supporters into the fold. But this work is not just for one person, or even for one department. The work of collecting, gathering, and disseminating stories is the responsibility of the entire organization, small or large. I hope you will take a moment to share this book with your colleagues. Storytelling and social media done in a silo will not get you the results you seek, nor the results that you deserve.

As we take this journey, you will see sprinkled in each chapter a variety of sidebars with tidbits of extra information:

◆ *Definition:* Describes language or terms of art specific to the subject area.

◆ *Example:* Clarifies a point.

◆ *Food for Thought:* Something that challenges old ways of thinking.

◆ *Important:* You guessed it, it's something essential to know, or important!

◆ *Observation:* A point worth calling attention to.

◆ *Practical Tips:* Information applicable to the subject area.

◆ *Principle:* Highlights a principle relevant to the subject area.

◆ *Quotes:* Advice or insight from an outside authority.

◆ *Stories from the Real World:* Using real-world examples to reinforce a point.

◆ *To-do Lists:* Bulleted to-do lists to help you put things into action.

◆ *Watch Out!* Vital warning to avoid a damaging or unexpected result.

Please feel free to contact me directly if you have questions, thoughts, ideas, or feedback on this book and this topic. I look forward to helping you on your storytelling journey!

Part One

Making the Case for Storytelling

In this first section, we will set you up for success when using digital storytelling strategies by looking at the concept of storytelling as a necessary marketing and fundraising tactic. We will discuss how to find the right people to involve in this process and provide a step-by-step guide to creating goals and objectives for your storytelling efforts.

Chapter One

We Are All Storytellers

IN THIS CHAPTER

- ···→ The definition of storytelling
- ···→ Real-world examples of compelling stories
- ···→ The benefits of sharing your stories
- ···→ Qualities of a stellar nonprofit storyteller

When you think of storytelling, what comes to mind? A campfire, a group of children sitting around a teacher, a few close friends chatting over glasses of wine or bottles of beer? For me, I think of my nighttime routine with my seven-year-old daughter and two-year-old son. We read at least one children's book, usually two or three, every night together. Even though they both love books, they prefer the nights when I tell them a story from my own life, especially stories from when I was a child.

A daily routine of sharing stories together helps us reconnect after a busy day and relate what we learn from the story to our everyday lives. It gives my children a better understanding of who I am as a person, and it helps them to see that I went through many of the same experiences (although, with not nearly as many Barbies and Matchbox cars).

Storytelling is not only a fantastic way to relate to other humans on a personal level, but it is also a fantastic marketing and fundraising tool. When done strategically and in harmony with online channels like social media, storytelling can and will help you accomplish the goals of your nonprofit.

All nonprofit professionals and volunteers need to start thinking of themselves as storytellers and not "executive directors," "development directors," or "board members." A comprehensive marketing and fundraising plan is of no use without the gasoline of good stories to fuel it.

In this chapter, I will cover what is generally meant by the term "storytelling" in a nonprofit context, the basic structure of a story, the benefits of storytelling for nonprofits, and the qualities of a great nonprofit storyteller.

What Do We Mean by a "Story"?

Human beings think in stories. We attend movies and plays, we read novels, we watch TV, we tell each other about our lives and our struggles. We express ourselves by telling stories. Stories have existed since the beginning of time as a way to connect people and to relay important lessons. They are also a way to ensure that important lessons from history will not be forgotten.

Great stories transcend cultural differences and language and make us understand the innate humanness in all of us. Think about the tragic love story of Romeo and Juliet. That story has been told millions of times in millions of different settings because the main themes of love and tragedy continue to resonate with people across all demographics.

A great story has what is called a "narrative arc": a beginning, a middle, and an end. There is a protagonist—the subject with whom the audience is going to identify and follow through to the end. There is also an antagonist—the obstacle or challenge that the protagonist faces, also known as the villain. The antagonist or villain does not need to be an actual person. It can be the loss of a job, the death of a family member, or a surprise illness.

An example of a story that your organization may tell could go like this:

Beginning: Our protagonist, Single Mom Susan, works at a corporate retail chain and goes about her day-to-day routine with her smart and precocious seven-year-old daughter, Grace. Susan works hard and makes many sacrifices so that Grace can get a great education as well as take dance classes on the weekends.

Middle Part 1: Out of nowhere, Grace starts feeling tired and sick. She is taken to the hospital where she is diagnosed with leukemia. The moment she gets the horrible diagnosis, Susan's life begins to fall apart all around her. She can't afford the medical bills and can't get paid time off from her job to take Grace to all of her doctor appointments. Susan lives across the country from her family members and has no outside support to help her.

Middle Part 2: Through a coworker, Susan hears about *your organization*, The Helpful Nonprofit. The Helpful Nonprofit provides transportation to Grace's appointments as well as vital help with child care and career training, which results in Susan finding a better paying job with more flexibility.

End: Grace is doing better and getting the treatment she needs, but there is still a long way to go. Susan, with the continued support of your organization, is upbeat and hopeful that things will get better for her family.

The Good, the Bad, and the Ugly

Remember that stories about those you serve do not have to be 100 percent positive and candy-coated. Don't hide your dirty laundry. Don't tell a bland, "vanilla" story.

The reality is that the work that you do every day entails fixing messy, complicated problems and alleviating real struggles. Your donors need to understand that these challenges are very real and require their attention and involvement.

In telling your stories, the protagonist should cause people to think twice and to ask themselves, "If I were in this situation, what would I do? How would I handle it? And how can I help this person overcome it and attain a happy ending?"

principle

The Reader Should Help Write the Ending

The purpose of sharing Susan and Grace's story is three-fold:

◆ It sheds a bit of light on what your organization does (that is, you help families in need). Hopefully, this will help others who may not have known about your range of services to seek your organization's assistance.

◆ It is a story of an individual family and not a large, unnamed group of people with whom the audience cannot identify or visualize.

◆ The story is one with which many families can empathize, especially if they have suffered hardship or illness in their lives. Thus, it will inspire people to get involved through volunteering, giving donations, or by sharing the story with others. Who would not want to help Susan and Grace?

Important note—A great story does not always need to have a picture-perfect ending! Sometimes, too-perfect endings don't ring true. The key is to be authentic and to choose a story that will resonate with your audience.

The best stories should also compel people to insert themselves into the story to help write the ending. After hearing or reading this story, your audience should be asking, "How can I be a part of creating a happy ending for Susan and Grace, and others like her? What small or large action can I take to help?"

Benefits of Storytelling in the Digital Age

There is a myriad of benefits that can be gained through a strategic online foray into storytelling—benefits that will resonate throughout the entire organization, from donors to clients to staff. Here are just some of the many benefits that your nonprofit will enjoy when you start using stories in your communications and fundraising efforts:

The Software Made Them Do It

On August 13, 2014, Jodi Kantor of the *New York Times* published a provocative piece about Janette Navarro, a twenty-two-year-old single mother and barista at Starbucks. The story described in excruciating detail the chaos and disarray in Navarro's life and the life of her four-year-old son, Gavin, caused by inconsistent scheduling practices at her job. Without being able to rely on a set schedule, and often getting less than twenty-four hours' notice of changes in her schedule, Navarro was unable to plan regular child care and a predictable budget.

The villain of the story was the company's practice of using scheduling software to cut costs (a common practice in many national retail and restaurant chains) at the expense of the workers. Due to the intense, personal story of Navarro and her son and the subsequent outcry on social media, the very next day Starbucks announced changes to the way it schedules its workers. More national chains followed suit.

Had Kantor simply written an academic article about the software and how it's used, I doubt that the nation would have paid attention, let alone mobilized and spurred changes that will now have a positive effect on millions of working parents like Navarro.

stories from the real world

Seeing Your Mission with a More Critical Eye

Yes, we know why we do what we do and why people should donate, volunteer, and attend our events, but can we tell it in a way that will make complete strangers care?

Collecting and telling stories out in the open forces nonprofits to answer uncomfortable but necessary questions. Most importantly, the sheer amount of information, both online and off, competing for your donors' attention should cause nonprofits to dig deep into the vital question, "Why should anyone care about what we do?"

Can you make people care deeply about your mission? So deeply that they will actively share your good work with others? Can your message cut through the clutter and the noise on the Internet? And if not, what are you doing wrong, and in what specific ways can you improve?

Increased Media Attention

Medical and law journals love dry statistics and research. Human beings and mainstream media outlets love stories. If you want to get in *The New York Times* or your local paper, having an interesting or unique story can lead to increased media coverage for the organization.

Bigger Financial Commitments from Donors

Donors are giving you their money, and they want to know that they are affecting change in real lives. Stories about the population served by your organization strengthen the bond with donors and can inspire them to share your good work with their peers.

If your nonprofit is to survive, you must have a comprehensive donor relations program—one that involves research, stewardship, acknowledgment, and cultivation. Social media and storytelling play an integral part in these four steps. They assist nonprofit staff in making personal connections, conveying impact, and learning more about who supports your program.

Word-of-Mouth Marketing

Telling compelling stories that get shared via social media exposes your nonprofit to new people. Your board of directors is constantly asking you, "Where can we find new donors and supporters?" The answer: Online!

When a supporter shares a story posted on your Facebook page or retweets your tweet, the supporter's friends, family members, and social network connections become aware of your organization. This helps you in your quest to spread the word about your programs and services to new people who may need them, as well as to people who may advocate for your cause.

Standing Out

Social media tools enable a nonprofit to provide a richer and more comprehensive picture of itself and its mission. There are so many hundreds of messages competing for our attention every second. To combat information overload, use stories. Videos and photos that tell the story of your organization add up to a much more interesting experience for a potential supporter. Stories told via Facebook or Instagram are certainly more eye-catching and memorable than a black and white photocopied annual report (and may even be cheaper due to printing and mailing costs).

Making Better Communicators

Great nonprofit storytelling requires creativity. Our culture values stories told in visual and emotional ways. Nonprofits everywhere are making a significant impact on the lives of others, and they have stories to tell. Tell them uniquely and compellingly without being boring or predictable.

Increased Transparency

Storytelling forces nonprofits to be transparent, which I love. Nonprofit naysayers and critics often have a problem with the supposedly secretive, "ivory tower" world of most organizations, especially larger ones. Storytelling through open social media channels allows you to lift the veil and be transparent in your operations and your work. This helps the sector as a whole be seen as authentic and truthful.

Instant Feedback

Social media provides an amazing way to communicate with donors in real time. Pew Internet found that, as of January 2014, 74 percent of online adults eighteen years of age and older use social networking sites. In fact, 73 percent of online adults eighteen+ years of age use at least one social networking site *daily*!

The lesson: Learn where your donors are already networking online and insert yourself into the conversation. Make your donors smile when they see the results of the gift they gave and the outcomes they directly helped to achieve.

Stay at the top of donors' minds with frequent Facebook postings, tweets, and Instagram photos that showcase the stories of your organization. Once you get in the groove and the social media mind-set, you won't be able to stop!

Social media tools are perfect avenues to gather instant, unfiltered feedback on a new program, topic, or question as well as validation and confirmation of your important work. Post, tweet, and share online and then listen to the conversation that ensues!

Characteristics of a Stellar Storyteller

Now that you understand some of the benefits of combining the powerful one-two punch of great stories and social media, what qualities do you need to be an effective storyteller?

Stories Cannot Stand Alone

Beware the "shiny new toy" syndrome. The terms "storytelling" and "social media" are trendy and mostly misunderstood. As a result, stories alone are not enough. Storytelling is a great strategy to convey the impact of your work, but it is not a panacea. You must be able to back up what you are doing or show that this is a real problem and you are answering a real need.

There are limits to the magic of storytelling for your nonprofit. Several things that storytelling and social media cannot do are:

◆ Fix bad management or incompetence

◆ Repair a lousy program or service

◆ Erase a bad reputation or public relations scandal (In fact, it may just amplify it.)

◆ Replace other marketing strategies that work for your organization

◆ Replace tried-and-true fundraising tactics, like direct asks and one-on-one meetings

◆ Cut the time you spend on marketing and fundraising in half

But if done well, a combination of storytelling and social media will augment all other communication and fundraising efforts!

practical tip

Great storytellers have a few characteristics in common. Not everyone will embody every characteristic on this list; they are simply guidelines to which you should aspire as you begin your journey to stellar storyteller.

Be a True Believer in the Cause

Stellar storytellers are outspoken and passionate advocates. Their zeal and enthusiasm are infectious.

Be Authentic and Truthful

We tend to want to listen to others with whom we can see parts of ourselves. People that come from similar backgrounds and have faced similar obstacles. This is why major donors tend to listen to other major donors and volunteers are better able to recruit other volunteers. They speak each other's language, know the hidden "codes," and understand where the other is coming from.

Truly Understand What It's All About

It's not about your organization's agenda and what you want to convey. It's about your audience members and what they want to hear. A stellar storyteller takes the time to understand the audience members. What they care about and what moves them. Stories should be crafted and delivered with these elements in mind.

Prepare, Prepare, Prepare

Preparation is key when delivering a great story. Stellar storytellers are also able to improvise and are not rigid in their delivery.

Practice Being Open-minded, Enthusiastic, and Motivated

Stellar storytellers want others to feel what they are feeling and they will always try new methods and new techniques to reach that end.

Remain Skeptical

Stellar storytellers continually ask themselves the questions that their audience will be asking: "How did that happen? Why did that happen? Why couldn't something else have happened?" By looking at each story with a critical eye, they are able to anticipate the apprehensions and questions of their critics and supporters.

Remain Generous

Stellar storytellers are generous with their emotions and their willingness to be vulnerable. They often share personal stories of their own struggles and obstacles. To touch other people's hearts, you must be willing to expose your own.   ✳

Understand the Context and Your Audience

Are you telling the story in front of a group of one hundred people, at an intimate dinner, or during a Reddit AMA? Molding the story to fit the context and your audience is a huge part of being successful in storytelling (more on this in **Part Three**).

It's all an exchange. Supporters give us their time to listen to or to read the story, and they expect us to deliver. Time is a very scarce resource for   ✳ people. Respect it, and they will remain loyal to you.

To Recap

- ◆ Stories help people relate better to each other, more so than facts and research.

- ◆ The best stories will compel people to insert themselves into the story to help write the ending.

- ◆ There are many benefits of storytelling on social media including bigger financial commitments from donors, increased media coverage, and deeper connections with supporters.

- ◆ Stellar nonprofit storytellers often have certain characteristics in common with a passion for the organization being the most important.

Chapter Two

Culture Shift: Creating an Army of Storytellers

IN THIS CHAPTER

···➔ Why resistance to social media and digital tools is futile

···➔ How to overcome obstacles to storytelling

···➔ How to create an enthusiastic, educated army of storytellers

···➔ Tactics to motivate and empower staff and volunteers

In **Chapter One,** we covered the many benefits of nonprofit storytelling and the characteristics of a stellar storyteller. You may be thinking: Who *wouldn't* want to foster deeper connections with donors and supporters while using the power of Internet tools to spread the word about your work and your impact? However, to truly begin reaping the benefits of these storytelling efforts, you need to address any reasons that your nonprofit may be resistant to storytelling on social media in the first place. You need to respectfully confront any fear and skepticism about social media and storytelling with the aim of creating an organization-wide culture that embraces these tools and strategies. And, importantly, you need to realize that you cannot do this work alone!

In this chapter, I will detail some of the ways you can identify, recruit, motivate, acknowledge, and coordinate an informed and enthusiastic army of storytellers for your organization and your cause. Getting energetic, creative people into the fold and invested in the work of telling stories will help you reach new supporters and deepen relationships with loyal ones.

Working with a team of storytelling enthusiasts not only takes much of the burden off of you but it will also generate creative ideas, and it's fun!

Resistance to Social Media Is Futile

Nonprofit organizations have traditionally held their cards close when it comes to sharing their most intimate stories. There is a perception that, since nonprofits do great work all day every day, people should just be compelled to give money (and to continue giving, and giving, and giving).

Reality check: No one *owes* your organization money, no matter how worthy the cause. It is your job to break down the barriers to giving and, in this day and age of digital communication, the way to do that is through thought-provoking stories shared widely via social media and other tools.

There are many reasons why nonprofits do not effectively use social media to tell stories:

Fear of the Unknown and Expecting the Worst

Fearful of negative comments and criticism, nonprofits would rather not share program information online, lest they expose themselves to naysayers and critics.

We Are All Too Busy, Busy, Busy

Ah, the omnipresent "busy-ness" factor. We all have too much work to do, too many fires to extinguish every day. We do not need one more thing on our ever-expanding, to-do list, which we have to tackle with ever-diminishing resources.

"Just Let Us Do Our Work in Peace!"

One nonprofit client I worked with did not publish staff contact email addresses or telephone numbers on its website for fear that people would actually contact its staff members! This behavior contributes to an, unfortunately, common misconception of nonprofits as the "third sector"— that we are all silent martyrs, working for pennies, in an environment that is not readily transparent to the lay person.

The Boring Factor

Have you looked at your website recently? Have you subscribed to a nonprofit email newsletter only to unsubscribe immediately after receiving the first issue? Sadly, the majority of nonprofit communications are incredibly boring and easy to ignore, and many organizations seem resigned to this unfortunate reality.

The Sector Needs a Culture Shift

The nonprofit world needs to adapt an entirely new mind-set. The myth of the nonprofit professional as inaccessible is destructive and pushes away potential supporters. Instead of being at arms-length and distant, we need to pull supporters into our orbit. We need to educate them on the issues, our mission, and our work. To access and engage the next generation of donors, we need to meet them where they are and give them what they demand: Evidence that we are doing good. That we are accomplishing our mission. That we are moving the needle on the causes about which they care.

Creating a shift in culture and mind-set from closed to open via storytelling and social media will not just be something fun to do, but it will also be something without which your organization cannot live. If you approach this method of communication in a strategic, systematic, and thoughtful way, you won't just be spinning your wheels in the digital marketing and fundraising arena, and you will be able to answer your skeptics' concerns. (Maybe your board of trustees or your coworkers do not agree with the need to tell stories using social media or to even collect stories at all. In that case, please buy them each a copy of this book and highlight **Chapter One!**)

How to Create an Army of Storytellers for Your Nonprofit

Identifying and coordinating an army of storytellers all comes down to education, inspiration, and information. Let's get right to it!

Get Acknowledgment from Executives and Leadership of the Organization

First things first. Get the influential and powerful people in your organization on board. You may be surprised to find out that not everyone is enthralled with social media or believes in the power of storytelling.

So how to convince them? There are a few ways. Talk up the benefits of storytelling that we covered in **Chapter One.** Assure them that there will be adequate training and comprehensive policies in place to protect the organization and the clients. Make sure to listen to their concerns carefully. Many people are wary of social media and have heard horror stories of tweets and Facebook posts gone wrong. Social media skeptics may need a lot of convincing that this is the right direction. Others may not be convinced that storytelling and social media will have a high return on investment for the organization.

I find that conducting research and preparing a comprehensive plan ahead of time works wonders to assuage fears and skepticism. Think of presenting your case for storytelling and social media like you would your case for support in a grant proposal or to a major gift donor. Create a brief write-up of your plan for getting the work done, complete with action items, estimated budget, resources needed, time estimated—as much detail as you can provide. It doesn't need to be perfect, as things will undoubtedly change as the work progresses, but it's a start.

Also be prepared to provide examples of nonprofits that are using storytelling and social media to connect with stakeholders, promote their cause, highlight their results for clients and the community, and/or to raise money. Make sure to address skeptics' concerns respectfully, and promise to keep everyone updated on your progress.

Beware the Social Media Skeptic!

Social media skeptics tend to believe in two pervasive myths: Only younger people are on social media, and young people are not sharing any information of value.

Social media skeptics tend to view social networks as vehicles to post photos and videos of cats and celebrities and cannot conceive of these platforms as vehicles for social good. These assumptions are harmful and, when perpetuated, completely disregard the fact that people of all generations are expressing interest in issues about which they care using social networks.

Your donors are on social media right now, sharing experiences, reading articles, and connecting with others based on collective values and beliefs. Even the so-called "old guard" is getting online in droves and demanding more personal, inside access to the causes about which they care.

Pew Internet releases studies every year on Internet and social media use and age. Consistently, year after year, Internet users aged sixty+ are the fasting growing demographic on social networks. See more at *pewinternet.org*.

Eliminate Silos

Being successful in storytelling and social media requires eliminating departmental and individual silos. Program staff is just as responsible for accumulating and sharing stories as the development director and marketing intern. To be effective and get results, storytelling and social media *cannot be done by one person and one person alone.* A comprehensive strategy and plan must be embraced by the *entire organization*, paid staff and volunteers alike, if it is to grow, thrive, and succeed.

How can you get the acknowledgment and support of your entire organization? Form a storytelling and social media committee!

Identify Potential Storytelling and Social Media Committee Members

Make three lists. On the first list, write down staff members, volunteers, board members, donors, community members, and constituents you know that have some of the characteristics of a stellar nonprofit storyteller (see **Chapter One**). People on this list should be active and engaged in your organization as well as enthusiastic about spreading the word. They do not need to be tech-savvy or know how to code a website. Simple knowledge of social media platforms is okay.

Make a second list of people who seem to know all of the movers and shakers in your community. Who is very well connected? Who always seems to know what's going on before everyone else? These people will be very helpful in gathering timely and relevant content to post.

Make a third list of the people who are most connected to the organization's programs and the people you serve and/or benefit. Having program staff, volunteers, and clients on the committee will ensure that your storytelling strategy stays close to the ground and remains authentic. You want to showcase your accomplishments and the amazing impact you create and what better way to do it than to engage those who do the work every day, as well as those who directly benefit?

Ideally, your storytelling and social media committee will be comprised of a combination of people from the three lists without one group dominating. (As with any committee, make sure to consult with your executive director to make sure that there are no political land mines if you ask one person over another person.)

The key to a dynamic storytelling and social media committee is the inherent passion of its members. They do not need to have marketing, public relations, or technical knowledge at first. That can be learned. The most important feature they should share is their connection to and enthusiasm for your cause. It may take some time to find the best combination of people but thinking strategically and methodically recruiting will save you time and headache in the long run.

Write up a Brief Job Description for Committee Members

A sample storytelling and social media committee members' job description could be as follows:

◆ Members will actively participate in forming and carrying out the storytelling and social media strategy of the organization.

◆ They will attend meetings, bring ideas and creative energy to the group, and implement strategies as assigned. This includes keeping an eye and ear out for great stories that can be shared as well as engaging with the organization on social media platforms and inviting others to become involved.

Success Story

The unprecedented social media and storytelling success of the Barack Obama 2008 presidential campaign has become legendary. The campaign organizers used a story-sharing method called "Public Narrative," developed by Harvard professor Marshall Ganz.

Using this innovative method, Obama campaign volunteers would gather in small groups and share personal stories of what led them to the campaign, what challenges they felt were the most important facing the country, and common themes, values, and ideas. Using the seeds of these stories, the volunteers were better able to connect with voters on a grass roots, personal level.

Think about how your nonprofit can use this method with your storytelling and social media committee, at staff meetings, volunteer orientations, and board meetings.

stories from the real world

◆ Feel free to add your own wording and your own requirements. Make it fun and light! This is not the place to include lengthy legal policies and restrictions. You want this committee to be a place of encouragement and ideas. (You can cover the rules, restrictions, and formal policies of your organization at the first meeting.)

Get out There and Recruit!

After a list of potential committee members has been identified, work with another staff member or volunteer to recruit about eight to ten people from the list. Remember that, most likely, the people you are recruiting

---

Creating Your Committee, Step-by-step

1. Talk to your supervisor or CEO about showcasing the impact of your organization on social media. Get their approval and invite them to be on the social media and storytelling committee.

2. Identify and recruit committee members based on their enthusiasm for the cause, their excitement about the opportunities presented by social media, and their interest in finding and telling stories. Do not recruit them solely based on technical skills or knowledge.

3. Bring food to the first meeting. And maybe wine. The important thing is that you make the meeting light, fun, and interesting for the members. Host a raffle or a short contest or giveaway to start things off with a bang.

4. Provide training and materials to the committee members. Send regular communications to them explaining how they can help. Give them advice and tips on how to find and tell great stories, and address any obstacles or challenges that arise. Acknowledge all ideas and feedback and provide support throughout the storytelling process.

5. To further cultivate a storytelling culture, encourage all organizational meetings that you attend to start or end with stories—staff meetings, volunteer orientations, fundraisers, events, and training.

6. Tie storytelling and social media efforts with results. Share these successes frequently with the committee members. Celebrate and have fun!

to-do lists

lead very busy personal and professional lives, so you will have to explain the importance of this work and why it is vital to help the organization accomplish its goals.

One way of convincing potential committee members to join is by explaining that it takes a village to make a difference in the world—and that adage is also true for social media!

You can also emphasize the reasons that you are doing this work and the anticipated and desired results, not just the tasks involved. However, do not sugarcoat the fact that it will be just that—work—but it will be fun.

Explain the value of the work to potential committee members. Tell them that success in using social media to tell great stories will result in an increase in donations and revenue, access to new donor prospects and high-net-worth individuals, access to potential corporate partners, and interest in your programs from potential partners. It will also create word-of-mouth goodwill for the organization as well as the ability to hire and train more staff and serve more clients. These factors will serve to generate prestige for your organization as a reputable and impactful nonprofit in the region, leading to greatly enhanced media and community relationships and increased positive coverage in national media.

Give Your Storytellers the Resources They Need to Succeed

Bring the committee members together for the first meeting and make it really fun and upbeat. Invite current or past clients to share a personal story of how the organization impacted their lives. Share photos and thank-you letters from people served.

Think about creating a small budget for the committee. There may not be money now, so ask yourselves: How can the members fundraise or use their own technology and resources to help collect and share stories? Take an inventory of what storytelling equipment they can bring to the table—smartphones, tablets, scanners, or video editing equipment, among other things.

Create some brief training materials for the committee and house them online in an accessible spot such as Google Drive or Dropbox. You can also create a Google Group or Yahoo listserve to share resources, ideas, articles, and stories.

Your training materials should include helpful articles on how other nonprofits are using social media to tell their stories. It is vital to creating an accessible story bank. This is a place where the committee can post photos, videos, graphics, documents, and ideas to share with the group. These items may never be shared on social media, but they may provoke ideas.

Ask for a Monthly Commitment

Commit to meet at least once per month, in person or virtually. In-person meetings are more desirable, but if you have volunteers scattered across the globe, a conference call, Skype, or Google Hangout may be the most viable option.

At each monthly meeting, the members should each bring a story or a story idea to share with the group. These stories may never be used, and they may be confidential or very personal. Emphasize that just because they are shared with the committee does not mean they will automatically be posted on Twitter.

The point of this exercise is to get everyone into the storytelling and sharing mind-set. It is also to inspire the group at the beginning of the meeting. (We will discuss in detail the process of finding great stories in **Chapter Five.**)

Provide Hands-on Training

Hire a consultant to hold a storytelling workshop for the committee members. (See the discussion on how to hire a storytelling consultant in **Chapter Seven.**) After the training, ask the members to write down some social change stories that they have heard or witnessed, or stories from other nonprofits that have resonated with them. The stories shared in this workshop could be memories not only from their work with the organization but also from their own lives or what they have learned from other nonprofits. The point is to share the story, discuss it with the group, and ask questions like: What makes this story memorable? Is this something that can be shared? Are there things that we can learn from this story? Why do these stories work? Do they elicit emotions from your target audience?

You may need to ask leading questions to draw information out of the members. Not everyone has a storytelling mind-set. Some members may never have used social media for marketing or fundraising before. There should be no intimidation or criticism during brainstorming and story-sharing sessions. Never be dismissive—make sure the members feel empowered!

Make a point to regularly attend relevant webinars or professional development seminars in your area to become more familiar with storytelling tactics and with social media tools. Then pass on what you have learned to the committee members!

Use a Social Media Lens When Thinking of Stories

The committee needs to be constantly thinking of ways that the organization can use social media to accomplish its goals. The members may need to reframe their entire way of thinking about nonprofit communications in the digital age.

As we will discuss in more detail in **Part Three,** your Facebook fans, Twitter followers, and blog subscribers are under no obligation to read and respond to every post. Your audience members make split-second decisions every minute about what information they will read, discuss, and disseminate to their networks. The ball is forever in their court.

If your nonprofit is consistently uninteresting and your posts are not eye-catching, you will be ignored. Charities that understand how digital tools

---

Resources

My favorite resources for nonprofit social media and storytelling ideas, information, and training webinars are:

◆ CharityChannel: *charitychannel.com*

◆ John Haydon: *johnhaydon.com*

◆ Beth Kanter: *bethkanter.org*

◆ Nonprofit Tech for Good: *nonprofittechforgood.com*

◆ NonprofitReady: *nonprofitready.org*

◆ The Storytelling Nonprofit: *thestorytellingnonprofit.com*

◆ Meyer Foundation - Stories Worth Telling: *meyerfoundation.org/impact/stories-worth-telling*

You may find your own resources by searching the Internet for "nonprofit storytelling examples" or "great nonprofit social media posts."

practical
tip

have forever changed the way humans communicate will succeed. The ones that do not will fail to use the platforms effectively.

The good news is that each program, service, event, and activity at your organization can be repurposed as a social media post, tweet, photo, or video—as long as there is a good story behind it. Teach the committee to start seeing the work of the organization through a social media lens. Everyone needs to be writers, publishers, photographers, videographers— or at least think like them!

Make It Simple and Easy to Share and Engage

The committee chair should send out a weekly email to committee members with their top three tasks of the week. The tasks could be as simple as promoting one of your nonprofit stories on their personal Facebook profiles, retweeting one tweet from the organization, and/or sharing or commenting on a recent blog post.

If you want to promote a particular story or fundraising campaign, make sure to provide the committee members with all the details. Don't simply send a vague, generic email saying, "Help us promote this on Facebook!" You will want to write the actual Facebook post that you want them to share. Compose the tweet for Twitter (making sure to check the character count). Attach the photo for Instagram and provide the caption. Provide committee members with great graphics and compelling photos to include with their posts and always provide a link back to your organization website or blog.

Committee members can then choose to simply cut, paste, and share, or they can adapt the language to make it more personal. The key is to make the process of sharing on social media simple and easy—something they could do while waiting to pick up their kids at school or sitting and watching a TV show in the evening.

Keep up the Momentum

In your monthly committee meetings, encourage open discussions about the challenges faced by the group. What is working, what isn't, and how can we improve on what is being done? At the same time, showcase accomplishments. "This story and photo that Pam provided not only got 147 likes on Facebook but it also got us an inquiry from a potential corporate partner!"

Provide reports on metrics that are of interest to the committee such as increased website traffic, increased activity and engagement on social networks, and increased online donations that can and have resulted from the committee's efforts. We will dive into measurement and reporting of this kind of information in **Chapter Thirteen.**

Celebrate Successes!

It is important to regularly show committee members the results of their efforts. Tell them that all the posting, tweeting, and sharing has accomplished something positive. Reports to the committee could include increased information about website traffic, event sign-ups, an upward tick in online donations, or inquiries. Show them also that sharing their stories online has increased community and enhanced connections with donors and supporters. It's not simply about pushing out marketing messages.

To Recap

◆ Advocate for a new mind-set within your nonprofit that sharing information about the organization's good works will help increase awareness of your cause.

◆ Creating a comfortable, accessible culture where stories are shared openly is vital for nonprofit social media success.

◆ A storytelling and social media committee should be carefully selected and given the necessary training and materials to make committee members' jobs easy and fun.

◆ An effective army of storytellers always knows why they are telling the story and can explain the impact of their efforts toward the organization's goals.

Chapter Three

Creating a Storytelling Plan

IN THIS CHAPTER

···➔ How to define goals and SMART objectives

···➔ How to identify key audiences

···➔ How to create a message that resonates

···➔ How to create an actionable storytelling plan

In the last chapter, you formed your army of storytellers and provided your soldiers with the motivation they need to get the job done. You started to break down the destructive silos into which many nonprofit professionals fall and identified those who can most help you in the storytelling journey. This chapter will help you create an actionable strategy for your storytelling and social media efforts before you ever send a single tweet. A successful strategy will be able to prove that it has helped the organization achieve its goals.

In my experience, nonprofits are too focused on creating a Facebook page and "getting fans" before they even have a plan for how to use it and why. Too often, we focus on the tools first, without creating a map and a plan with which to use the tools efficiently. (That's why I don't even get into the tools until **Part Three!**)

I suggest a meeting with your army of storytellers to develop this strategy. An independent, objective third party such as a storytelling consultant is often necessary to keep things on track and to focus people's thoughts and ideas. (Remember the storytelling and social media committee that you formed back in the last chapter? This is the perfect place to utilize committee members' talents and ideas!)

Ask Yourself: Why Are We Doing This?

The first question that you need to ask in all of your storytelling and social media efforts is, *why?* Why are you doing this in the first place? In making this evaluation, you need to first determine where you are going (the goal). What is it that you hope to achieve? What will your organization look like one year from now if you are successful?

Then determine the road you will take to get there (the strategies). What actions do you need to take to get there in the most efficient way possible? The path you wish to take will help you identify the tools and tactics required to get there—the actual work to be done.

Is your nonprofit's main goal to get more donors? Acquiring new donors and keeping the donors that you have is a fantastic and admirable goal for your storytelling and social media efforts. However, when you go deeper, what does "getting more donors" mean? How can you accomplish it?

You need SMART objectives to help you measure progress toward your goal and hold you and your team accountable for each small step along the way. SMART objectives—detailed later in this chapter—are **S**pecific,

---

Perspective

A lot has been written about the pros and cons of measuring "vanity metrics." Vanity metrics refer to the number of fans or followers on your social networks. While measuring these numbers is important, the weight you put on them depends on your goals.

If you want to position your organization as a national leader in the field, having a large online community is definitely something you want to measure. However, having the "right" fans and followers on your social media channels as well as high engagement rates are much more indicative of your online impact and are of much more import to your cause and mission. Avoid exclusively creating objectives around vanity metrics. A large number of Facebook fans does not matter if it does not include the people you most want to reach.

Measurable, Actionable, Realistic, and Time-based. They will help ensure that you are on the right track and heading in the right direction.

Many nonprofits want to start telling stories on social media "to get ten thousand fans and followers." However, when creating your goals and SMART objectives, you need to dig a little deeper. Is this *really* your goal? Why do you need these ten thousand fans and followers? What will ten thousand online connections get you? How will spending time and money building your online community push the needle on the work you do every day?

Define Your Goals

Thinking through the "why" question will help you identify your nonprofit's goals. I do not mean the overarching, big-picture goals and vision of your organization, however. For our purposes, your goals should be focused *specifically* on why you are or plan to be using storytelling and social media for your nonprofit. Think about the priorities of your nonprofit for the next year. (You may need input from your board members on this.) Are you putting most of your resources toward program development? Growing your donor base? Increasing awareness around a particular program or service?

Warning: "Getting on Facebook" or "start tweeting" are *not* goals! They are the tactics and tools you will use to achieve your objectives and goals. (More on this in the next section.)

Sample goals for a storytelling and social media campaign include:

◆ To establish our president and CEO as a respected and sought-after thought leader in the field of early childhood education, which will help us advocate nationally on this issue

◆ To increase visibility and name recognition for the organization, which will contribute to bringing in more prospective donors and corporate partners

◆ To develop dynamic, engaged social media communities that best represent our overall constituency, which will help us achieve our mission of educating teens on the dangers of dating violence

Goals are bigger picture items—the things that you want to achieve that can be assisted by your storytelling and social media efforts. They may seem a bit fuzzy, soft, and hard to measure. Thus they need to be matched with SMART objectives, detailed below.

Choose Your Strategies

The strategies you choose are the ways in which you are going to accomplish your goal. Let's say the goal is to increase visibility and raise awareness for your organization. Strategies to achieve this could include: posting daily on social media sites, starting a blog, revamping the email newsletter and sending it out bimonthly, contacting regional and national media outlets via Twitter to see if they will write a story about your organization, and working with influential bloggers to get them to share our stories.

Creating SMART Objectives

We've all heard of SMART goals, but I prefer to create SMART *objectives*. SMART stands for **S**pecific, **M**easurable, **A**ctionable, **R**ealistic, and **T**ime-based. Objectives are the specific actions you will measure to determine if your strategies are succeeding. Objectives hold us accountable because they can be measured.

If your goal is to increase visibility and name recognition for the organization, your strategies should include using digital marketing and online tools. Sample SMART objectives might be:

A Word on Tracking Progress

Achieving your goal of increased awareness and visibility can best be measured in the increased reach and size of your social media communities, traffic to your website, and email subscribers. Each of these metrics indicates increased interest in your organization but do not tell the whole story. You will also need to measure qualitative and anecdotal data—that is, board members who say they saw your stories online, prospects who let you know that they heard of your nonprofit via Facebook, and the like. It is essential that you take note of all of the times these things happen!

Short of conducting comprehensive pre- and post-surveys with your target audience, you will never know exactly how or if you have achieved your desired level of name recognition and visibility. But being clear about benchmarks from the beginning and measuring them along the way will let you know that progress has been made and that you are on the right track.

important

- To increase the number of fans and followers on the organization's social networks by 25 percent in six months

- To increase the organization's reach on social networks by 25 percent in six months. (Reach refers to the number of people that see your posts and tweets.)

- To increase the number of email sign-ups received by the organization by 25 percent in six months

- To increase traffic to the organization's website by 50 percent in six months

- To increase the organization's media placements and inquiries from the press by 25 percent in six months

If your goal is to develop dynamic, engaged social media communities, then you will want to keep track of engagement numbers. Engagement is very different than the number of fans and followers you have. It refers to how many times your social media community members have taken action on a particular social media post.

Strategies for this goal may include conducting research via social media on the organization's target audience, creating a content marketing plan tailored to the organization's audience, and connecting with influential people on social media that have a connection to the organization's cause or mission.

Sample SMART objectives to measure engagement numbers might be:

- To increase the engagement rate on the organization's social networks by 50 percent in one year. (Engagement is measured in the number of likes, shares, comments, retweets, and the like. It will be different based on the tools that you use to disseminate your stories.)

- To increase the number of shares of the organization's stories on social media by 25 percent in six months. (Shares are important to measure how your stories are resonating. If people take the time to share them with their own networks, it is working!)

- To increase the number of blog comments by 25 percent in six months. (If your blog readers are taking the time to thoughtfully comment on your blog posts, this is a good sign that they are paying close attention to what you are saying.)

Define Your Key Audiences

Defining key audiences that you want to target via your storytelling and social media efforts is often challenging for nonprofit organizations. Unlike corporate businesses, who may only have one or two key audiences (customers and trade journals, for example), nonprofits serve several distinct constituencies—donors, volunteers, staff, clients, community members, and partners. This broad variety of audiences often requires different information and, sometimes, conflicting methods to reach them.

There are three main benefits of identifying key audiences for your nonprofit organization:

◆ The ability to create targeted storytelling and social media campaigns, thus allocating time and resources more efficiently

◆ Garnering a deeper level of engagement on social networks

◆ Increased website search engine optimization, known as SEO. (If you know who you want to visit your site, you will be better able to research what specifically will get them there and what will make them stay.)

The most important thing to remember when determining your key audience is that "everyone in the world" is not a key audience. Not every person in the world, or even in your small community, will understand and care about the stories your nonprofit has to tell. Remember Seth Godin's wise words: "If you need to water down your story to appeal to everyone, it will appeal to no one."

Having multiple audiences for a nonprofit is expected. For example, a nonprofit event venue would market the same space in completely different ways for weddings than for business parties, or an alumni association might take different fundraising approaches for college students than for business executives. The key is identifying these audiences, prioritizing them based on your goals and objectives, and determining what you need them to do to accomplish your goals. The more important the audience to your goals, the more resources you should dedicate.

For example: If raising $1 million is a goal, then your key audience is *donors* (and high-level donors at that). If increasing enrollment in a particular program is a goal, then the key audience is *clients*. I am willing to bet that most of us want to raise more money or increase awareness of our cause and our organization with an audience that can give us money. So let's start there.

When defining the characteristics of your key audience members, in this case *donors*, ask yourself the following questions:

◆ Who is most likely to take this action—that is, become a donor?

◆ What are their passions and interests?

◆ What are their dreams and goals?

◆ What are their personality characteristics?

◆ Are there any difficulties or barriers that you might have in communicating with this audience?

Consider the following factors in defining your key audience members:

◆ Age group

◆ Location (local, regional, national and/or urban, suburban, rural)

◆ Marital/family status

◆ Income level

◆ Educational background

◆ Occupation

Then, think deeply about their motivation and why they are involved or would get involved with your organization. Ask yourself:

◆ What's their self-image?

◆ What are their day-to-day worries and goals?

◆ How are they trying to create a meaningful life?

◆ What behaviors are they trying to change?

◆ What motivates them to share information with their networks?

Then think about where and how your organization fits in. Ask yourself:

◆ What do these people already know about you?

◆ What value do you provide? (You need to shift the conversation from *how they can help you* ("Donate! Volunteer!") to *how you can help them* (making them feel like they've made a difference).)

◆ How does your program help?

◆ What problem does it solve? (For donors, think about this as how it makes them feel.)

◆ How does it make their lives easier? Better?

◆ What else would motivate them to get involved?

◆ In their words, what are their reasons for helping your organization?

When defining a key audience such as donors, you also need to think through exactly what you want them to do. In this case, the action that you want to elicit is a donation (or an email sign-up to get communications about donating in the future). Ask yourself:

◆ What may drive them to take the action that you want?

◆ What influences your donors to take that final step?

◆ What obstacles might be in their way? (This could include a bad website, complicated donation process, and no impact stories.)

◆ How can you eliminate the identified obstacles?

Where Does Your Key Audience Get Information?

Now that you have a pretty good idea about your donors' background, values, hopes, dreams, and motivation, consider where they get their information. It could be from the magazines they read, TV and movies they watch, websites they visit, and the social media sites they frequent. Then consider how they usually find out about you.

Thinking about where your donors are consuming media and information is a vital step in creating the tactical plan for getting your stories out there. It will require some research on your part, but it is well worth it.

Create Your Key Messages

Now that you have identified your goals, objectives, and the audience that you need to reach to achieve success, let's focus on creating the messages that will resonate with that audience.

The first thing to remember is: Not every audience gets the same message! Your clients are interested in different information than your donors and volunteers, and the media requires different motivators than your staff.

If one of your key audiences you want to reach with social media and storytelling is potential clients, think about the messages and ideas that members of this audience need to hear to convince them to participate in your program. Most likely, they care less about the history of the organization and its impressive track record than they care that it's safe, clean, and confidential.

Once you identify your key messages, you can then determine the types of stories that you need to collect that correspond with each message.

Key Messages for Potential Clients

A past client of mine was a prestigious college access and success program that focuses on career fluency and building professional networks. Its clients are high school and college students, so it would need a message that will resonate with these students as well as their families.

Sample messages could read:

◆ We will help you set and attain your college-to-career goals.

◆ We provide high-quality, real-world advice and training on how to build and sustain a personal and professional network because we passionately believe that this is a vital skill not taught in school.

◆ We partner with high profile, experienced leaders in the community to provide this training and to help you start your own network.

◆ You will become part of a supportive team, honing your skills and learning in a safe and empowering environment.

Key Messages for Donors

This educational/professional organization also aims to use its storytelling and social media plan to connect with more donors and business leaders in its city. The messages to that audience would be different. These would read:

◆ We provide high-achieving, underserved students with the skills to achieve their college-to-career goals. This is an investment in your business's future/society's future.

◆ We are a well-respected and trusted organization with a proven track record of helping students succeed. Eighty-nine percent of our graduates complete college in four years, and 85 percent of our graduates secure a career-track job or admission to a graduate program within six months of completing their undergraduate education.

◆ Root Cause, a Cambridge-based nonprofit research and consulting firm, conducted a comprehensive and independent analysis of our program and other college and success programs in Boston and gave us thirty-one points out of a total of thirty-five. This establishes us as a *high-performing* program, the highest category given by Root Cause.

Key Messages for Media

Another audience that is going to help this nonprofit reach its goals of increased visibility and thought leadership are influential writers, bloggers, and the media. This key audience not only cares about the impact of the nonprofit but also anything that makes it stand out or any tidbits that would make a great news story. These messages could read:

◆ We are much more than a traditional after-school program for underserved students. Instead of focusing solely on getting kids into college, we work intensively with students all the way from college preparation through the entire college experience to starting a career or graduate program after they graduate.

◆ We have worked with prominent thought influencers and business leaders such as Bill Gates, Sheryl Sandberg, and James Dimon.

◆ We have a proven track record of changing lives and creating opportunity. Eighty-nine percent of our graduates complete college in four years, and 85 percent of our graduates secure a career-track job or admission to a graduate program within six months of completing their undergraduate education.

See the slight differences in these messages? The main point of this exercise is to get you thinking of your audiences as individuals who care about different things, not just a group of general contacts lumped together to whom you reach out once in a while with generic, uninspiring messages. Some of your messages may stay the same or be tweaked only slightly, as there may be overlap in the interests of your key audience groups.

Fill in the Work Plan

Now that you have your destination and a way to measure your progress, how are you actually going to get there? Start by writing down each of your objectives on a separate piece of paper. Then list the tasks that you need to perform to achieve each objective. You should also assign roles to these tasks and a deadline by which they should be completed. If they are ongoing tasks, write "ongoing" next to them.

Sample objective: To increase the number of fans and followers on our Facebook page and Twitter account by 25 percent in six months.

Task	Person(s) Responsible	Deadline	Notes
Create storytelling calendar with list of upcoming events	Social media committee	October 1	Set up a committee meeting
Choose five topics to explore more fully and develop into stories	Sally	October 5	Talk to program directors to get access to clients
Get visuals or photos to accompany each story	Sally	October 10	Make sure to get proper permissions
Look at Facebook Insights to determine best times to post	Jane	October 15	
Look at Twitter Analytics to determine best times to tweet	Jane	October 15	
Explore purchasing social media ads	Mike	November 15	Find out if there is a budget for this
Ensure that social media links are in all staff email signatures	Mary	November 20	
Start posting daily on Facebook and Twitter	Jane, Mike	December 1	Evaluate what types of posts our audience likes best—photos, videos, links?

There are many more tasks are necessary to accomplish the sample objective detailed here, and I have only listed a select few. You will find that there will be multiple and varied tasks under each of your objectives. If the amount and scope get too overwhelming and exceed your staff or volunteer capacity, revisit the objectives to determine which ones get the highest priority. Table the others.

Be reasonable and realistic in your expectations of what can be achieved. Is an objective of doubling our Twitter followers in three months actually achievable if you do not have a dedicated staff person managing the Twitter account?

In upcoming chapters, I will help you fill in the blanks by giving you story ideas, identifying places to find great stories your donors and supporters will love, and providing several storytelling and editorial calendar templates to help you manage it all.

To Recap

- ◆ Before jumping into any social media channel, you need a plan of attack and a reason for being there.

- ◆ Create SMART objectives, rather than relying on vague, big-picture goals.

- ◆ Defining your key audiences and tailoring your messages specifically to those audiences is vital to communicating the proper stories that will elicit action on their part, be it via like, share, retweet, a monetary contribution, or otherwise.

- ◆ Continually evaluate your SMART objectives based on the number of tasks they require. Do you have the organizational capacity to do it all?

Part Two

Building Your Storytelling Arsenal

I n this part, we will cover the specific types of stories that you need to collect and share as well as places to find great stories and ways to encourage people to share their stories and experiences with you.

Chapter Four

The Stories You Need to Tell

IN THIS CHAPTER

- The six most effective and engaging types of stories nonprofits must share

- Practical tips and tricks to collect, refine, and share stories from your community

- Best practices and real-world nonprofit storytelling examples

In the first part of this book, I made the case for nonprofit storytelling on social media. I encouraged you to convince your colleagues of the importance of collecting and sharing stories to aid ongoing marketing and fundraising efforts. If you were very productive, you might even have changed the culture of your nonprofit to one that actively embraces and celebrates storytelling!

At this point, you should be motivated and enthusiastic about collecting, refining, and sharing the stories that show how your nonprofit ticks. You may have a few questions, such as: Where should I start? What types of stories do I need to collect? Where do I find them? How can my nonprofit tell such a great story that it will compel people to take action?

There are many, many types of stories and even more ways to share them, so the possibilities can seem endless and overwhelming. In this chapter, I will discuss the six most effective and engaging types of stories used by nonprofits to help you separate the wheat from the chaff and get focused. Keep in mind that you should be telling these stories everywhere you connect with donors and supporters (especially online and social media channels, as discussed in later chapters).

The Six Best Types of Stories for Nonprofits to Share

There is a misconception in nonprofit fundraising. Nonprofits tend to believe that donors give their time and treasure to the organization itself. However, donors are actually giving *through* you—the nonprofit—to make a difference on an issue that matters to them. You need to continually prove that you are a good steward of their donation and that you are actively working toward a solution to the problem or in furtherance of the mission.

Communicating with donors and stakeholders a few times annually, or even once a month, does not suffice anymore. (Did it ever?) People want and expect to understand where their money is going. Younger donors especially are demanding more of a firsthand experience from the causes they support. They want to see the direct impact of their giving and want to get to know better the people and places where they are effecting change.

Telling several different types of stories about your work, staff, volunteers, community, and beneficiaries will address the knowledge gap between the organization and the supporter. Here are six different types of stories that your nonprofit needs to be collecting, crafting, and sharing.

1. Impact Stories

Too many nonprofits go about their work every day only saying how many people they fed or how many applications they helped fill out. Doing the work is definitely important but to what end? What is the result? And how can you convey the impact in a story?

Impact stories are the most important stories you can tell about your nonprofit, but they are not actually about you at all! They are about the people, animals, or environment you have helped. They are about the lives you have changed. How has the world been improved because your organization is serving it?

Stories about the outcomes of your work are by far the most valuable weapon to have in your storytelling arsenal. Donors, volunteers, staff, and community stakeholders all want to know what impact your organization is having on the problem. Impact stories will make them feel like they are part of the mission being accomplished.

Questions to ask when creating impact stories:

◆ Are you actually effecting social change? In what specific ways?

◆ How can you showcase the impactful work you are doing through those that you have helped?

◆ What would happen if you closed your doors tomorrow?

Impact stories can feature some data points ("We served 1,250 meals to hungry children this year"), but they should not be data-driven. Effective impact stories feature one person or one family whose life was changed by the work you did for them. Lives saved, animals sheltered, research funded, environment cleaned, kids taught. All of these are outcomes of which your donors and supporters want to feel like they are a part.

Because they can be challenging to create, too few nonprofits share their impact stories. We don't like to pat ourselves on the back and congratulate ourselves for a job well done. Let's change that. I will go into greater detail on places to get impact stories in the next chapter.

2. User-generated Stories

User-generated stories are those generated by your community—your donors, volunteers, staff, and supporters. These are the storytelling gold standard as they are often shared widely across social networks and increase exposure for the organization.

Using Instagram

The organization charity: water uses Instagram to tell its impact stories in fifteen-second videos and compelling photos. It often features a story of one woman in the field or one family whose life has been completely changed by having access to clean drinking water.

The best feature of these stories is their rawness and authenticity. Often taken with smartphones, the videos and photos do not rely on fancy props, staged backgrounds, music, or narration to get their point across. The emotion conveyed by a child drinking clean water for the first time is enough to show the impact. To see more of charity: water's compelling visual storytelling, visit its Instagram page at *instagram.com/charitywater.*

Example

Getting stories from the outside is much easier said than done. Just placing a call for stories on your website or sending out an email usually is not very effective. People are incredibly busy, and their attention spans are short. How can you get them to actively participate by creating and sharing their own story with you?

Tips for getting user-generated stories:

◆ *Make it very easy.* Try to avoid a complicated submission process with a list of fifty rules and regulations in tiny type. Unless it is a contest or sweepstakes and you need their information in case they are the winner, do not ask participants for personal information at all. Simply have a place online where they can upload or post their stories or create a specific hashtag where you can search for their stories on social media.

◆ *Be where they are.* Ask for stories where people already are (most likely, on their phones and on social media). Keep the process simple. Have people submit their story via email, Facebook, or Twitter. That way you only have to monitor three places. Find out where your target audience spends its time and go there first.

◆ *Provide an incentive.* Holding a competition or a contest with a great prize can really motivate people to share information.

◆ *Spread the word.* If you have a database of contacts, send your contacts a special letter and email informing them about the new campaign to get user-generated stories. Post about it on your social networks and promote it at all events.

◆ *Acknowledge and thank!* It takes effort, time, and courage to share a personal story. Make sure that everyone who participates gets a personalized thank-you and public acknowledgment.

3. Values and Ethics Stories

Your donors and supporters want to better understand your organization to make sure that you have shared values and ethics. By expressing your values and ethics through a story, you demonstrate what is at the root of your organization. Examples of nonprofit core values include but are not limited to integrity, excellence, empowerment, honesty, and embracing diversity.

Value stories allow new people to immediately identify with your nonprofit and figure out if it's for them. (Reality check: As awesome as you are, your nonprofit isn't going to resonate with everyone. Sorry!) The main reason people get involved with specific causes is that the cause and the organization embody their morals and values. I am not going to donate to a cause that harasses people and bullies potential supporters. But others may find that approach effective and in line with what they believe to be moral and ethical.

We know that donors give to your charity based on shared values. Think about ways in which you can convey your unique values and beliefs to supporters.

A great example of value and ethics storytelling can be found on the Environmental Defense Fund (EDF) website, *bit.ly/EDFStory*.

EDF was created by a small, passionate group of conservationists on Long Island who wanted to save the osprey, bald eagle, and peregrine falcon. This dedicated band of people fought hard and eventually got the harmful chemical DDT banned in Long Island in 1966, and subsequently played a large role in the nationwide ban.

By reading its value story, supporters can immediately identify with its history of perseverance against all odds, its willingness to fight for the underdog, and its continued commitment to grass roots organizing.

Make It Fun

Get your online community members to share photos that feature their kids, a group of people in funny costumes, or several people parodying a popular TV show. The more creative you are in creating a fun contest, the better response from your community.

Best Buddies International—the world's largest nonprofit organization devoted solely to providing opportunities for friendship, employment, and leadership development for people with intellectual and developmental disabilities—used a series of creative photos to ask its Instagram followers to use the new Best Buddies mobile app to submit their news and updates. By doing so, participants would be entered to win a prize. Best Buddies frequently posts fun and light-hearted photos and stories on its Instagram account and receives above-average engagement from its committed online community. To see its original and engaging photos, visit *instagram.com/bestbuddies.*

Example

4. Social Proof Stories

Social proof, also known as social influence or herd behavior, is the tendency of individuals to assume that the crowd knows best. This is why you may choose the restaurant with the longest wait over the other restaurant with no one in it. You assume that others know more than you do. Indeed, social proof is the reason that businesses and charities alike vie to get famous celebrities on board with their latest campaigns. The thinking is that if a household name like Angelina Jolie supports it, it must be worthwhile!

Even if you don't have an A-List celebrity touting your cause, social proof stories can be effectively used by your nonprofit to leverage support. Ask yourself: Who are your most vocal supporters? Which influential community members have been moved by your work?

How to Collect Social Proof Stories

Three ways to collect and tell social proof stories are:

◆ *Trying local sources.* You may not have nationally-known staff and board members, but I'm willing to bet you could get the mayor, a state senator, or a local TV news celebrity or sports figure to explain why they support your nonprofit. (And if they don't know about you, make them know.)

Using Quotes

The St. Baldrick's Foundation does not provide direct services to cancer patients and their families; it funds childhood cancer research (a somewhat dry topic). To make its social media posts more compelling, St. Baldrick's features heartfelt stories from the volunteers who make up the lifeblood of the organization—the brave souls who shave their heads every year and collect sponsorships from family and friends.

Sharing these inspiring stories helps make the idea of shaving one's head for charity more accessible and in turn motivates more people to participate, either by making a donation or holding their own individual fundraising event.

To read more of St. Baldrick's volunteer fundraiser stories, visit Facebook.com/StBaldricksFoundation.

Example

◆ *Collecting stories from funders.* Funders, like directors of large foundations and major gift donors, like to hear from other people that run in the same circles. If you have a longtime donor vouching for your organization to other donors, this is a much stronger reason for support than if you are just tooting your own horn all the time.

◆ *Coaching these storytellers.* Have influencers or local celebrities tell their stories of how they first became involved with your nonprofit. Ask them to discuss the main reason they are passionate about your cause and the work that you do. Why do they believe your nonprofit is vital to the community and what enhancements have been made possible because of it? You will need to coach these supporters a bit by asking provocative questions and getting the conversation rolling.

Offering donors and supporters social proof stories will make them sit up and take notice and further compel them to get involved, especially if you are a small, community-based nonprofit without a broad base of support.

5. Founder Stories

I know that the founder of your organization has a great story to tell. Otherwise, why go through the hard work of starting a nonprofit? Let the

---

Working with Celebrities

One of the most widely-celebrated social proof campaigns has been coordinated by the It Gets Better Project. Its mission is to communicate with lesbian, gay, bisexual, transgender, and questioning (LGBTQ) youth and let them know that there are hope and support for them around the world.

In its ongoing campaign, It Gets Better Project enlists LGBTQ celebrities to tell their personal stories of coming to terms with their sexual orientation. The heart-wrenching and intimate stories detail the challenges that the individual celebrity faced along the way and provide words of hope and support for others that may be in the same situation. In these emotional videos, the celebrities endorse the work of the It Gets Better Project and list ways that a viewer can get directly involved.

Example

world know the story behind your founder or founding members. In getting information for this story, you need to ask the following questions:

- ◆ Why was your organization created? What need did it fill or address?

- ◆ Who identified the need and when?

- ◆ What was that like for them?

- ◆ What were their struggles in the beginning?

- ◆ What did they sacrifice?

- ◆ What did they gain?

It is important to get the founder's or founding members' permission before sharing such a story. They may be reluctant to be in the spotlight, and that is certainly their right. However, if you can show examples of other nonprofits using their founders' stories to connect with their audiences and supporters, your founder or founding members will probably come around.

The global education nonprofit Pencils of Promise features its founder's story prominently on its website, *pencilsofpromise.org.*

Adam Braun founded Pencils of Promise in 2008 after an eye-opening trip to India. He was inspired by a young boy begging on the street whose only wish was for a pencil. There is much more to his story, but the beginning draws you in and makes you want to learn more. Understandably, people deeply empathize with Adam's touching story, and they identify with the thinking behind his idea. This makes for a strong connection to the organization and a more loyal supporter overall.

6. Journey Stories

Sharing examples of a nonprofit's journey (also called "learnings") are all the rage in funding circles. Showing that you aren't perfect and that the organization is willing to be fluid and flexible is important to many donors. Sticking with the status quo just because you have done it that way for fifty years isn't going to impress many people. Telling me the ways in which you learned and changed as a result of an obstacle or failure— now that's exciting!

To think through possible angles for a journey story, ask yourself:

- ◆ In what specific ways can you show your supporters that your nonprofit is continually learning and improving?

◆ Did you start out in one direction and then discover a different, greater community need?

◆ How have you adapted to the needs of your constituency throughout the years?

◆ What challenges have you recently faced and how did you overcome them? Or not?

Examples of journey stories can be found online in The Denver Foundation's video series, *10 Years 10 Stories* (*bit.ly/DenverStories*). The Denver Foundation created a series of videos depicting real-life stories from nonprofits who were awarded grants. Most organizations would solely focus on the positive and the grant recipients with stellar outcomes where everything went as planned. Not in this series!

Not all the grants and programs worked out the way they were intended, but the best part of each story is how the nonprofit leaders discuss what they have learned and what still needs work. Supporters of the foundation's work leave feeling like the stories haven't been sugarcoated and that they want to be involved with the work to see it to its conclusion and help with improvements along the way.

I created these six categories to provide you with a framework within which to begin collecting the stories around you. Your nonprofit will undoubtedly have more types of stories to share and ones that do not fit into these categories. I encourage you to write down all possible types of stories to find a good mix, rather than relying on just one type of story.

To Recap

◆ The six categories of stories that nonprofits should collect and share are impact, user-generated, values and ethics, social proof, founder, and journey stories.

◆ These stories should be collected with an eye toward creating a deep, personal connection with a potential donor or supporter.

◆ User-generated stories are the hardest to get but lead to the most engagement by an online community.

◆ Your nonprofit staff, board members, and volunteers should be telling these stories wherever donors and supporters are listening—online and offline.

Chapter Five

Places to Find Great Stories Your Donors Will Love

IN THIS CHAPTER

- ····➔ Where to find great stories
- ····➔ How to involve your donors in storytelling
- ····➔ How to convince and empower people to share their stories
- ····➔ How to ensure a steady stream of stories to share

As described in **Chapter Two,** transforming the staff, volunteers, and supporters of your organization into an army of passionate storytellers involves changing an entire mind-set and culture. It's not easy, but it is important. Everyone involved in storytelling will have to shift from the predominately organization-centric mentality that permeates the nonprofit sector to one that is donor-centric.

Keep in mind that your supporters require a variety of stories (some ideas can be drawn from the six categories discussed in **Chapter Four**) to keep them interested, enthusiastic, and motivated to stay involved. So where do you, the nonprofit professional tasked with this (and many other pressing tasks), find compelling stories?

Thankfully, there are many places to find stories—even if you think you don't know where to look. But gathering up great story ideas is only half the battle. When you find these story ideas, how do you convince people to share them with a wide audience? And how can you plan ahead to make sure that your online communication channels are always stocked with great donor-centric content? In this chapter, I will get you well on your way to collecting and crafting stories that you are able to disseminate far and wide. I will help you create a storytelling calendar to help organize your efforts and to ensure that the well never runs dry.

Places to Look for Story Ideas

In the last chapter, I covered the six types of stories you should be telling about the people that you serve and the people who make up your organization. This should give you a good base from which you can start your story-collecting efforts.

Think like a Journalist

A journalist always has an ear to the ground and eyes peeled for the next great scoop even when not technically on the clock. Think about the journalists you admire and the news stories that catch your eye. What do they have in common? How can you take parts of that and incorporate it

---

Demonstrate the Bigger Picture

Stories alone are often not enough to convince people to get involved with your cause. You must be able to prove that your organization is addressing a time-sensitive problem and answering a real need in the community or in the world.

Once you establish a connection with a supporter through an emotional story, explain that this problem is not relegated to one individual or even one type of individual. Highlighting individuals or small groups of people in your stories helps to establish empathy with donors, but they may also need hard data on the problem to be convinced it's a cause that needs their immediate support. By showing the data and the numbers—how many people suffer from domestic violence each year, for example—you are proving that a need for your solution exists.

The Michael J. Fox Foundation and Mercy Corps are examples of charities smartly using data and financial information to support their great storytelling.

into your story hunting? Then, who would be the lead characters? What evidence would you collect? Who would you interview first?

Get up to speed on national and local news especially as it relates to your particular issue and cause. You never know where a story idea may spring up. Make sure to monitor relevant news sources and related organizations on social media to see what they are sharing. The "Trending" news feature on Facebook and Twitter is a great place to start.

Look over Your Printed Materials

In the course of your organization's history, it is very likely that you have produced a plethora of collateral materials—brochures, letters, website text, grant applications, event programs, and the like. Comb through these existing materials for content that could be repurposed and used in storytelling.

Your mission statement could be turned into a story. Your vision statement, strategic plan, and other documents that are undoubtedly sitting on a shelf gathering dust can and should be revived and repurposed. You do need to get creative, but you don't have to reinvent the wheel constantly.

Examine Your Events

Chances are you have had quite a few fabulous event speakers and emcees through the years. Look over those guest-of-honor and award-recipient lists. Even if these people were not directly served by your organization, you can get their stories about being involved and use their experiences in your storytelling.

Remember Your Smartphone

If you have a phone with photo and video capabilities, use it everywhere you can. Bear in mind that just because you *take* a photo or video does not mean that you are required to post or share it. Indeed, taking photos and videos is a great way to spur creativity, remind yourself of a story idea, or just catalog the day's events to refer to later. Be wary of taking photos or videos without the subject's verbal or written permission (even if you have no intention of sharing it publicly) and never, never share this material online without the proper permissions.

Brainstorm

Remember that storytelling and social media committee that you helped create back in **Chapter Two?** Have committee members text you with ideas on which you can follow up. Keep the lines of communication open—share story ideas via email, social media, Skype, and good, old-fashioned face-to-face meetings over coffee. Encourage the committee members to submit every idea no matter how impractical or underdeveloped.

Get on the Front Lines

Get out from behind your desk! Attend a support group, serve lunch at the food pantry, go on a volunteer mission. Immerse yourself in the real work of your organization. When you get your hands dirty and dive deep into the programs and services around you, you will undoubtedly find fantastic stories.

Send out a Survey

Poll clients, alumni, partners, volunteers, and staff. This can be done online, in a small focus group, or informally at a staff luncheon. The survey can be anonymous if you prefer but make sure to ask for contact information if people would like to speak to you later. Even anonymous sources will provide story ideas on which you can follow up later with others who are willing to go public.

Don't Forget the Staff!

Staff stories are some of the most compelling. You never know what gems could be hiding in your own backyard. Catalog the "behind the scenes" of a big fundraiser, advocacy campaign, or program opening. Talk to staff about why they started the work, their personal journey, and their hopes and dreams. The nonprofit staff are some of the most dedicated and passionate people in the world—capitalize on this unique feature of the sector.

Keep Those "Thank-you" Letters

If your nonprofit has been serving the community for a while, it is sure to have amassed a lot of thank-you letters. Take a look at these for story ideas and for people to contact. The letters may be from the local third-grade class thanking you for a tour or from the mayor thanking the organization for decades of service. There is a story in each letter. Take some time to pour over them and see what could be expanded and what is worth exploring further.

How to Involve Donors in Storytelling

Stories do not have to feature only the direct recipients of your services. Consider your donors, the people who are making your work possible every single day! As we learned in **Chapter Two,** donors should be represented on the storytelling and social media committee. They have a unique perspective about why they give and donors tend to listen to other donors when making donation decisions.

Talk with your most loyal funders, foundations, corporate partners, event sponsors, board members, people who donate in-kind, and more. Find out what giving to your organization has meant to them. When calling donors, give them a chance to share a small anecdote about why they have decided to support your organization. Put a short note in appeal mailings and thank-you letters, encouraging donors to come forward with their stories.

An example of a great donor story can be found on The Findlay-Hancock County Community Foundation YouTube channel. In this short video, a donor discusses in detail how her family and her history impacted her

Making It Personal

Many nonprofits—both small and large—have encouraged their supporters to share personal stories via their website and social media:

The McCormick County Library in South Carolina asked for stories from its users to celebrate National Library Week. But it didn't ask for stories just for the sake of more public exposure. It explained on its website that user stories can and do make a real difference in securing government funding for public libraries statewide.

Planned Parenthood asked a simple question on its website: "How has Planned Parenthood been there for you?" Encouraging people to share such personal stories is difficult, but Planned Parenthood emphasized that each story would encourage others to seek treatment and also help its legislative advocacy efforts.

On Father's Day, Macmillan Cancer Support in the United Kingdom asked people to share three words about their fathers, using the hashtag #thatsmydad. These ministories were sometimes hilarious, sometimes heartbreaking, but always interesting and entertaining. As we learned above, by creating a hashtag that appealed to a variety of people young and old, Macmillan was able to expose its mission and its organization to a very broad group of potential supporters.

stories from the real world

decision to support her community through philanthropy. Watch it here: *bit.ly/FindlayDonor*.

How to Convince the People You Serve to Share Their Stories

As a nonprofit professional, you have to tackle tough situations every day. However, there is no doubt that hearing about the impact that you have had, straight from the heart of real-life people, is the most vital piece of the storytelling puzzle. One of the hardest tasks may be convincing the people that you serve to share their experiences on the record and in public. You need to come off as persuasive and convincing, but not smarmy and inauthentic. Here are eight tips to encourage clients to share their stories:

Empowerment and Listening First

This is incredibly important. Listen to your clients and the people who benefit from your programs and services. Make them understand that receiving help from your organization is not the defining event of their life. They have a lot more to offer and as the song says, "The rest is still unwritten."

Ask: What are their hopes and dreams for the future? Do not just discuss the hard times that brought them to you for help. Do not interrupt or interject your two cents. Listen and listen some more. Offer support and let them know that your conversations do not have to be on the record or shared with others. Even if they had initially said that they would be willing to have their story shared widely, respect their decision to change their mind.

Explain How the Stories Will Impact Your Work

It is important to let a potential story provider know that stories from actual people about personal, authentic experiences have the benefit of encouraging others in similar situations to be more comfortable in seeking out assistance from your nonprofit and in helping your organization better connect with people who want to support the work of the organization. Both reasons are equally important and should not be downplayed when recruiting people to tell their personal stories.

Connect with the Story Provider Regularly

Make sure that you consistently provide moral support to those sharing their story and let them know they can pull their story at any time. Just because the story has been used in one blog post or tweet doesn't mean it can't be taken down upon their request.

Provide Examples

People often think that their individual story isn't interesting or unique or compelling. Show them examples of other stories you have collected or that other organizations have used. Explain that all stories are valuable to the organization. Even if the story is never used officially in a video or publication, it could lead to more ideas and more storytelling inspiration.

Provide Training

Never assume that those who share their story are comfortable speaking in front of a group or a camera. They may need assistance in getting their story down on paper or in a blog post format. Meet them where they are and always be willing to offer help and support as they need it. Simply saying, "Send your story to me via email," may not work for everyone. Understand the limitations of those telling their story, and encourage them to share their experience and thoughts in a way that feels most comfortable to them.

Additionally, if the person providing the story is being enlisted to do public speaking such as at a fundraiser, you may need to connect the storyteller with professional training resources. If the story will be on video, coach the storyteller as necessary.

Follow-up

Always follow up after the story is collected and published to let the story provider know that they are valued. Explain how the story is making a difference. The worst thing you can do is reach out to a client for a story and never contact the person again after you collect it!

If You Can, Get More People on Board

If some your storytellers seem willing, encourage them to recruit others to do the same. See if they would also be willing to be kept on a special list of people willing to speak to the press, speak at public events, write blog posts, and the like.

Consider forming a support group or a training group for those who want to regularly help your organization by sharing their stories. If they are willing, ask them to join the storytelling and social media committee to provide their unique insight and perspective.

Lead by Example

The leaders of your organization should be heading the charge to find and share stories about your impact. How can the CEO and the board president inspire others to come forward with their experiences?

How to Coach People to Be Great Storytellers

Human beings are natural storytellers! Think of the last time you went out to eat with friends, or called a family member, or browsed your social media feeds. Our interactions with each other are made up of stories; it's how we can relate our experiences to others. Also, people tend to enjoy talking about themselves and their experiences. They may not enjoy public speaking, or being on video, or even writing things down, but they most likely will share something about themselves if the circumstances are right.

The key to coaching the people around you to be great storytellers is to exploit the natural human tendency to relate experiences through stories and to leverage the pleasure others get when talking about things from their perspective.

Start by finding the right people. Choose the "low-hanging fruit" first—the people that you know can and will share their stories or are comfortable sharing others' stories (with permission). These people will become your greatest assets, and you can use them to train other potential storytellers at a later date.

Make your storytellers feel comfortable. Meet them in a familiar environment and get them to feel safe. Do not criticize, laugh at, or disregard any parts of their stories.

Speak honestly. Find out why others may be reluctant to come forward or to share publicly. Define the obstacles and then determine a course of action to overcome or address them.

Be sure to practice with your storyteller. The importance of practicing storytelling cannot be overstated. Even if you are only going to start by telling a story to your immediate family around the dinner table, practice and practice again.

Provide information to your storytellers. Make sure that your website and social media channels are updated with the most recent data and information on your organization and your cause. Provide resources to storytellers in the form of videos, bulleted talking-point checklists, photos, and graphics. These materials will allow your storytellers to craft a compelling story for the medium that they choose, whether it is a blog post, a tweet, or a personal email to friends and family asking for their support. Photos and videos are worth a thousand words especially in storytelling so make sure that you provide visuals to accompany all stories. Putting these resources online in an easily accessible format allows your storytellers access when they need them.

Before approaching people who may have a great story to share, think about their experience with the organization. Where are they coming from? Where are they now? If they are deeply connected to a particular staff person or volunteer, consider inviting them to the meeting or having them make an email introduction. Be sensitive to potential conflicts and issues and make sure you allow them plenty of time to get back to you if you are sending an email or leaving a voice mail. (Whatever you do, you want to avoid the last minute, "Hey, we have an event tonight for five hundred donors; can you come and speak?")

Before your initial discussion with a potential storyteller, think carefully about the questions you will ask and the information that you want to collect. What do you want the reader or viewer of the story to know and understand? What details could make this story even more compelling? Be cognizant that asking people to "tell your story" may intimidate them. They may not think they have a perfect "story" to share. Keep it simple. Try asking for an experience or a favorite memory while encouraging the person to share as little or as much as they want. Make sure you allow adequate time afterward to go through the questions, hone the story, and follow up on details that may need clarification.

When you meet with your storyteller, start slowly. Do not overwhelm people. Speaking in a small support group and standing in front of two hundred strangers at a gala event are two completely different things. Find out where they are most comfortable starting out. It might be a simple Q&A with you writing the blog post afterward or it may be a simple photo on Instagram with a short caption. Fit the tool and the platform around the person and the story, not the other way around.

Always acknowledge the hard work that goes into storytelling, give accolades, and share rewards generously.

How to Maintain a Steady Stream of Stories for Social Media

Getting one or two great stories about the impact of your organization is easy. The demanding work of collecting, cultivating, and creating stories that will feed the always-hungry social media machine is daunting.

To ensure that you never run out of story ideas, use your storytelling and social media committee members! That's what they are there for, after all. Take turns each week assigning members to story hunt and report back to you or to the group. Incentivize your committee members and others by instituting a storytelling challenge with special prizes and incentives. The winner is the person with the most innovative and unique story idea during the time period of the contest.

Most importantly, create a storytelling calendar. In your storytelling calendar, mark off important events and dates during the year when you will have opportunities to collect and/or tell great stories. Think about fundraising events, volunteer orientations, board meetings, organizational milestones and anniversaries, and important cause awareness days (such as World Cancer Day or Domestic Violence Awareness Month). Determine who will be responsible for which date or event and in what capacity. This way you are not scrambling at the last

---

Photo Essays for Good

The Denver Rescue Mission (DRM) showcases the life-changing impact of its work by collecting powerful client stories and matching the stories with photography. DRM then crafts social media posts featuring one or two photos and a short blurb introducing the story, enticing the reader to click through and read more on the site.

One example of this is in a series of photos that DRM posted to its Facebook page with the caption: "Most of John's life has been spent in and out of jail and when he ended up homeless, the only place he knew to go was Denver Rescue Mission. Read more about John's journey in our new Next Step program and how he was able to utilize the services he so desperately needed: http://bit.ly/DRMFebNewsletter."

For more examples of this kind of compelling storytelling using imagery, visit *Facebook.com/DenverRescue.*

stories from
the real world

---

minute to find someone to document a major event or activity. Using a storytelling calendar will also help you plan backward to adequately coach a potential storyteller to speak at an event or participate in a video, depending on how much prep work is required. A sample template of a storytelling calendar is located in **Appendix A.**

To Recap

◆ Look for great stories to tell within your organization (founders, executives, staff, volunteers) and outside of it (donors, community members, clients).

◆ In formulating story ideas, look at current events and issues related to your cause, thank-you letters from constituents, and your own mission statement, to name a few.

◆ People who want to share their personal stories need to be empowered, not strong-armed.

◆ Creating a storytelling calendar will ensure that you are consistently and regularly collecting and sharing relevant, timely stories in accordance with your nonprofit's goals.

Chapter Six

Stories That Turn People from Passive to Active

IN THIS CHAPTER

- → How to drive your donors, supporters, and online fans to take action through compelling storytelling

- → How to move people from passive to active supporters

- → How to write a succinct and compelling "call to action"

The power of storytelling, video, and social media connected me to the Kibera School for Girls. A news organization that I follow on Facebook posted an update from Shining Hope for Communities, the nonprofit that runs the school. The video features Eunice, a fifth grader who lives in Kibera, Kenya, and her incredible poem about persistence in the face of unimaginable challenges.

I immediately fell in love with Eunice since I have a smart and spirited young daughter of my own. I shared the video everywhere, and I began supporting the school and teaching my daughter (and soon, my infant son) about the challenges faced by girls trying to get an education in Kenya. The video can be found at *bit.ly/EuniceStory*.

If I had tried to explain the plight of these girls with data, an academic report, or a dry news story, it never would have opened the eyes of my friends and family. They had to see and hear Eunice and other girls like her to truly understand and empathize with the cause and thus be moved to support it.

In previous chapters, I explained that, as a human being, you are a storyteller by your very nature. As a nonprofit professional, you need to be a great storyteller to convey the impact of your work in a way that everyone can understand (and hopefully get excited about). How can you create your own "Eunice's Dream" video or story?

Of course, this is much easier said than done, as is pretty much everything worth doing. You know you need to craft compelling narratives to entice donors and to cut through the noise on social media but how to do it? What if you are not a writer or videographer? The good news is that all of us have the capacity to tell a great story. In this chapter, we will cover the basics of telling a high-quality story that will leave your supporters wanting more and taking action.

What Are the Elements of a Great Story?

By now you know the types of stories that you should be collecting (**Chapter Four**). You also know where to look for these stories (**Chapter Five**). After you write down all of these ideas from a variety of sources, how do you mold them into effective narratives? More importantly, how do you create stories to which your supporters will actually pay attention?

In a nutshell, nonprofits should be using their stories to motivate the reader or the viewer to do something. This "something" is referred to as a "call to action"—the action that you want a person to take after being emotionally triggered by your story. If you are telling stories with no call to action (or CTA), then what is the point? You will be hard-pressed to measure the success of your efforts without a particular CTA.

For example, a call to action can be making a donation, filling out a petition, or calling a legislator. Bear in mind that there should only be one call to action per story or you risk diluting the message. Ideally, the CTA would be an action that you can measure yourself via social media shares, video views, increased email sign-ups, event registrations, and the like.

Great stories also inspire and motivate people to share them with their friends, family, and personal networks. Taking action through the CTA and sharing are the two holy grails of social media and storytelling and should be the dual goals of any storytelling campaign.

Getting People from Passive to Active

Motivating supporters to act on a CTA requires purposeful efforts that will inspire them to share a story, retweet information about your organization's good deeds, and donate funds or resources to support the organization's latest efforts.

Focus on Your Target Audience

This will not only help you craft an effective story but will also serve to guide your CTA. Great stories resonate with their *target* audience. The word "target" is critical. As we discussed earlier, the reality is that no matter how wonderful it is, your nonprofit story is not going to make a difference to everyone in the world. It's not even going to appeal to everyone that supports your cause. You have to first define your key audience and craft a story that will appeal directly to it.

To do so, think first about your supporters and your most passionate advocates. Referring back to the strategies discussed in **Chapter Three,** remember to ask yourself:

◆ What do they like?

◆ What do they have in common?

◆ What moves them?

◆ What makes them sad, happy, angry?

◆ What is most important to them?

As you answer these questions, the story will begin to take shape. Determining your key audience is a crucial element in using storytelling and social media tools effectively.

Think like an Educator

A great story should also serve to educate the audience members and provide them with information that they did not previously have. It will give them something fresh and interesting to take away and hopefully share with another person or group.

Start by asking:

◆ What is the problem being presented?

◆ What are some frequently asked questions about this problem?

◆ What are some persistent myths or stereotypes that need to be addressed?

Addressing myths and misconceptions about the people you serve is a great way to figure out the trajectory of the story.

Think like a Donor

Nonprofits should always be viewing their communications through the eyes of their donors. In fact, the donor should be the hero in the story. For example: "Because of your support, we were able to provide one hundred meals to homeless veterans this winter." Or, "Because of your continued investment, we built a new playground in a part of the city with little to no outdoor recreational space."

You also need to consider other constituencies and audiences—advocates, volunteers, clients, and media contacts, to name a few. Each group will have different motivators and story lines that work best to get them to take action. Think through your communication plan, going back to your goals and SMART objectives to help determine the best and most powerful CTA for each one of your target audiences.

How to Get Your Donors Involved in Writing a Happy Ending to the Story

I am fortunate to work with the Urban Scholars Program at the University of Massachusetts Boston. With college enrollment and completion at the heart of its mission, the Urban Scholars Program serves academically talented middle and high school students (ages thirteen to nineteen) from predominantly low-income and underrepresented backgrounds.

In our thank-you letters to funders, we always include a great story about one of our scholars who has found success but is still in the program. We want donors to feel connected to the student and invested in the student's success, and understand that the student's story is not over and that the program still needs funding to help the student in the journey to college and beyond.

In this way, we are getting our funders involved in writing this student's story. We are asking if they will continue to help ensure that our program is fully funded and able to offer high-quality services to the student and their peers. This is conveyed to the funder, along with our sincere appreciation for their support and the positive impact they have made in our students' lives.

stories from the real world

Create a Story Series

Many nonprofits have multiple constituents to serve and a wide variety of programs and services to offer. They are simply unable to encompass all the great work that they do in one, thirty-second video clip. Maybe this sounds familiar! I am here to tell you that, while you may have ten different programs serving ten different groups of people at your nonprofit, you cannot tell all of these stories at once, in one video or in one social media post. The reality of today's cluttered communications landscape means that bite-size stories, often called "snackable content," work best across online platforms.

To maximize the impact of your storytelling efforts and to fit into the short attention spans of your audience, focus on just one central topic per story. Less is always more when you are asking people to take an action! The best way to create these "snackable" stories, while still ensuring that you cover all the important bases, is to create a story series.

A story series is a collection of your best stories and testimonials told from several different angles and perspectives. One story would focus on a client or a person that benefited from your program; it would tell about the person's experiences. A second story would be told from the perspective of a staff member or the executive director. A third would feature a volunteer or board member and cover the reasons that they remain committed to the organization. And so on—the possibilities are endless! A story series is perfect for sharing on your website, blog, and social media channels, ideally in short-form video format or a sequence of short blog posts.

Mix up the Emotions

Remember the famous and on-point quote from Maya Angelou: "I've learned that people will forget what you said, people will forget what you did, but people will never forget how you made them feel."

It is important to keep in mind that all of the stories you share do not have to leave the reader or viewer warm and fuzzy inside. The reality is that often the resolutions to problems are not neatly tied in a bow. People face challenges and struggles along the way and are maybe still facing them. The important thing is to mix up the emotions conveyed by each story. Create a story that will make people feel anger, sadness, hope, or happiness. Getting people "passionately inspired or pissed off," as Chelsea Clinton has put it, is the key to getting their attention and convincing them to take action. The worst thing that your story can do is be forgettable or leave the audience apathetic.

Be provocative, be interesting, be unique, be emotional. It's the only way to survive in the hypersaturated, rapid-fire social media landscape.

Highlight Involvement

Your donors and supporters give "time and treasure" to your organization because they want to be involved in creating a happy ending for those you serve. With your story, show outsiders and potential supporters how they can be a part of writing a happy ending, either through donating, volunteering, or advocacy. Think of the story as convincing them to enter into a partnership. This is where the call to action comes in—how can they help after they have been inspired?

> ### Visuals Are Vital!
>
> As mentioned in **Chapter One,** Visuals rule the digital world, and we all know that photos are worth a thousand words. Videos, infographics, collages, memes, and the like all add up to a much more in-depth and interesting experience for a potential supporter. Additionally, visually compelling social media graphics are certainly more shareable than a black and white photocopied annual report (and cheaper due to printing and mailing costs). Always be thinking of creative ways to incorporate visuals into your nonprofit stories—through photos, videos, graphics, and original artwork.
>
>  practical tip

Focus on Your Impact, Not Your Organization

In marketing lingo, businesses are often asked to focus their messaging on "benefits" and not "features." Benefits to a consumer are simple: What do I get if I purchase this product? Features involve the nuts and bolts of a product. People have been found to care much less about the product itself—how it's made, what's in it—than the results achieved from it.

To translate these concepts to the nonprofit world, you need to ask: How has the community changed because of what you are doing? Do your donors feel good about supporting your work?

Benefits in a nonprofit sense are a bit more intangible to communicate but are still important. Your supporters are continually asking themselves: What impact is this organization having on my community, on the world? Will I feel good after supporting this cause? Will it reflect well on me to my network of friends, family, and work colleagues? They will say to themselves: Your programs are great and we are happy you are efficient but

Spontaneous Storytelling with "Caine's Arcade"

Seth Godin famously wrote, "Here's how to know if you're on the right track [with storytelling]: if you stop your story in the middle, the audience will insist you finish it." A great story is one that captures people's attention and makes them eager to hear the end! One of my favorite examples of this kind of storytelling is the viral YouTube sensation, "Caine's Arcade." The story has a fantastic narrative arc, starting when we are introduced to the adorable nine-year-old Caine Monroy. Caine's father cannot afford to send him to camp in the summer, so he spends his days in his dad's used-autoparts store in East LA.

Caine doesn't feel sorry for himself. Instead, he uses his incredible imagination and creative skill to construct an arcade entirely out of cardboard boxes and other supplies he finds in the store. This sets up the story and helps us empathize with Caine and begin to root for him. Despite the poverty surrounding him, Caine's resourcefulness and entrepreneurial spirit cannot be dampened. He is hopeful that he will have arcade customers one day. And the viewer is hopeful right along with him.

Nirvan Mullick, a filmmaker, came into the store one fateful day, simply seeking a door handle for his car. He discovered Caine's Arcade and became its first customer. Nirvan was so inspired by Caine's creativity and determination that he decided to make a short film about the boy.

In the middle of the story, we see the challenges that Caine faces. His father discusses how business is down as there is a lack of walk-in traffic in the neighborhood. Thus, Caine has trouble finding customers for his brilliant arcade. Much to the viewer's delight, Nirvan and Caine's dad plot to surprise Caine with a flash mob of customers. I challenge you to watch what happens when Caine sees the crowd and not tear up!

Then we come to the end of the narrative arc, eagerly asking, what comes next for Caine? When he created this film, Nirvan hoped to raise $25,000 for Caine's college fund. He did not set out with the intention of creating a movement. However, the overwhelming outpouring of support and international reaction to Caine's Arcade inspired the creation of The Imagination Foundation, which has raised over $250,000 for Caine's Scholarship Fund. You can watch the story of Caine's Arcade here: *cainesarcade.com*.

stories from
the real world

tell me an individual story of someone who went through your program! I see too many videos about Fabulous Nonprofit X having been around for 155 years. They will also say to themselves: Well, that's all well and good, but has it made a tangible difference? Your donors are asking these questions and expecting you to answer them in advance. You'd better answer them through your storytelling.

Employ a Clear, Concise Call to Action

You have created a story that elicits an emotional response. It is virtually guaranteed to make people step up and want to participate in the great work of your organization. So now that you have their interest and attention, what are you going to ask them to do? It will be hard to resist asking them to donate, while also asking them to "like" you on Facebook, sign up for your email newsletter, and add your specific hashtag to all of their tweets. In my years of experience in nonprofit communications and fundraising, one direct "ask" is all to which most people will respond, given the demands on their attention at any given time.

Remember, you are competing for their consideration with all the other distractions in their lives—children, smartphone notifications, work emails, television. Your supporters do not read or view your story in a bubble of complete silence.

There are two vital characteristics of any compelling call to action. First, all CTAs need to be *crystal clear* about their requests. What specifically are you asking me to do? You have mere seconds to communicate this and to get someone to click. Use powerful action words like "Donate," "Give," "Help." Incorporate a sense of urgency into the "ask," but keep it short. Think of people viewing the CTA on their phones, unsure of whether to act now. Compel them to take action by making it very clear what will happen when they do decide to click on that link or that "Donate" button. No surprises here!

The second feature of a great CTA is that it is absurdly *easy* to accomplish. Even if you think it may be easy, review the process with someone not close to it—I am willing to bet you can make it even more simple. For example, in an email solicitation, you craft a compelling CTA for donations. As an interested donor moved by the story shared in your email, I am inspired to click on the brightly-colored "Donate" button included in the email text. But instead of a form where I can enter my credit card information, I am taken to the main page of your website. I now have to wade through multiple web pages before finding the donation form. Chances are, something will distract me in those precious moments, and I will click away.

Think carefully about each step required in completing the action requested. Put yourself in the shoes of your donor. Ask yourself: Do I have to fill out a huge, cumbersome registration form with multiple fields before I can make a donation? No time right now; maybe I'll do it later. (Chances are, you won't.)

Always be considering ways to streamline and remove any obstacles between what you are asking people to do and how they can actually do it. Interest and attention are incredibly valuable resources in today's time-strapped, busy world. Don't waste them by not carefully thinking through the process.

Incorporate Data, but Don't Let It Be the Focus

In **Chapter Five,** I mentioned the importance of including some backup data in your storytelling. As you know, data and statistics are useful to prove that you have had demonstrable success in accomplishing your mission. It is also important information in showing that you are solving a real problem in the community or in the world. For example,

Real-life Stories Work Wonders

The St. Baldrick's Foundation is a national charity that funds cancer research for children with the disease. Its website is chock-full of compelling stories about the children and families who have been directly affected by its funding initiatives.

On its blog, it has an entire category of "Real-life Stories," all told from the perspective of the family or the child suffering from cancer. At the end of each blog post, there is a short, simple call to action, usually referencing the child who has been helped:

Help kids like Ben. Contribute to lifesaving childhood cancer research today. Give.

When you click on the brightly-colored "Give" button, you are taken directly to the online donation form, not to the main page of the website or another page with a list of ways to get involved. St. Baldrick's is making the assumption that people clicking on the "Give" button are ready to get out their wallets and give money—and it is making it extremely easy to do so. Read more of its Real-life Stories on its website: *stbaldricks.org/blog/category/real-life-stories.*

 stories from the real world

if college access and success are your focus, how many students have you helped enter college and matriculate? How can you tell the story of David, who achieved success, while asking the reader to help support the many others like David?

When using data in storytelling, think about reshaping it to make it more interesting and jaw-dropping. Giving percentages and using visuals to provide data in a clearer, more understandable way is ideal. Instead of saying, "Malaria kills one child every thirty seconds and about three thousand children every day. That is the same amount that attends full day kindergarten in our local town," tell a story about a family who was devastated by malaria and how your organization is helping to ensure that fewer children die every year until the number is zero.

Don't Use Jargon

"We focus on place-based initiatives to alleviate poverty, empower disadvantaged populations, and inspire community action."

I just made that up, but it is certainly not hard to imagine a nonprofit writing a mission statement exactly like it. Often, nonprofit professionals cannot get out of their heads; they want to cram so much into a mission statement that it ends up meaning nothing.

Jargon is the death knell for communications in general, but especially storytelling. Stories are designed to grab people's attention and inspire them. Do not spoil this feeling or squander their time by using terms or acronyms that the average person will not understand. Think about wording the story as if you are telling it to a kindergartner. How would you explain it? Even complex themes can be expressed in an easy-to-process way.

To ensure that your story is relatable to people who are not familiar with your organization, try it out on friends, family, and even complete strangers. See what your supporters think of it. Ask them honestly if it would compel them to donate, volunteer their time, or answer a CTA. Use their feedback and learn from it to improve your storytelling.

To Recap

◆ Great nonprofit stories benefit supporters by showing them the organization's impact and benefit the nonprofit by inspiring new people to take an action on its behalf.

◆ Stories should consider the rational mind, but the emotional heart is the golden ticket. That's where you want to reach people to compel them to give or get involved.

◆ An effective story is one that people share with their networks and one that compels them to take an action.

◆ A clear, easy call to action woven into the story is vital to take your readers and viewers from passive to active.

Chapter Seven

Addressing Common Challenges in Storytelling and Social Media

IN THIS CHAPTER

····➔ Solutions to the most common storytelling challenges

····➔ How to address confidentiality restrictions

····➔ How to tackle resistance to sharing stories online

····➔ How to coach clients into becoming great storytellers

If you are reading this book, you understand that combining storytelling and social media is an important and vital way to raise awareness, deepen existing donor relationships, and grow new support for your cause. (Not yet convinced? Go back and reread the **Introduction!**) Authentic, genuine stories of real people in real situations make up the holy grail of storytelling and are the best way to demonstrate the impact of your work to outsiders.

However, even if you are personally convinced of the power and importance of storytelling and social media, you may be hesitant to broach the topic with your executives and colleagues. This is entirely normal. The good news is that it can be overcome.

It is true that some nonprofits face particular and unique challenges when collecting and sharing stories about their work on social media. In my work as the development and marketing director at a domestic violence prevention program, I came across numerous obstacles to collecting and sharing authentic stories of the families that we served. The safety and security of clients, legal issues around photo and video permissions, and lack of enthusiasm or participation from program staff are just a few roadblocks that you may encounter on your storytelling journey. This chapter details the six most common challenges facing nonprofits in telling their stories online and via social media—and my solutions.

Challenge #1—Our Organization Has Never Shared Stories Before

If your organization has always relied on pure data or vague conjecture in its communications, changing the status quo is going to be difficult. I'm not going to lie. Nonprofits like to remain in the background, never raising their hands and rarely seeking out accolades for their amazing work.

We also tend to think that our donors and supporters prefer us in the shadows, heads down and doing our work without fanfare or applause. However, this is a myth. Your donors want to see you at work with the recipients of your services—and their actions! They want to see the day-to-day, behind-the-scenes dirty work that makes it all happen. They want to congratulate you, celebrate your accomplishments, and most importantly, feel that they are an integral part of the impact that your organization is having on the world.

As discussed in **Chapter Two,** it is not impossible to change the culture of the nonprofit to one of openness and transparency. Not only is it doable but, in today's digital world, it's also mandatory. Remember that no one person or even one department can do the work of storytelling alone (at least, not well). You need an army of storytellers to support you, to help you flesh out story lines, and to reach out to clients and supporters of your program.

Your nonprofit may even operate with everyone in their own silo, hoarding information and resources. This often happens when the program staff doesn't communicate with the development staff and so on. Or the opposite may be true—you may be a lone wolf, the only person tasked with doing the work due to lack of resources, staff, and capacity at your organization.

Creating a culture of storytelling and an enthusiasm for sharing on social media requires training, coaching, and professional development for everyone involved in the organization. This includes volunteers, donors, staff, and board members. It also requires reaching out directly and personally to clients and others who have experienced and benefited from your programs and services. This is something that you may not be entirely comfortable doing and something to which program staff may not initially be open. However, to get stories, you need to change the closed-off, insular culture and encourage the organization to become more transparent and accessible.

Get outside help or professional development training when it comes to working together, gathering stories, and sharing them on social media. Hire a storytelling consultant or narrative strategist to work with you on changing the culture to one that embraces and encourages storytelling (detailed below). Start a storytelling and social media committee (detailed in **Chapter Two**) to support you in this work.

A nonprofit that openly shares a variety of stories about successes and challenges is one that shows donors and supporters that it's making a difference and it's always learning. That translates into being a good steward of funds and a great agent of social change.

Working with a Storytelling Consultant

If your nonprofit has never collected or shared stories about its work before, the situation may call for an outside consultant. In this case, a consultant may be hired to conduct staff and volunteer training on storytelling and to help create a plan of action for staff and volunteers to

---

Stories That Directly Help Others

Stories are often about more than just showcasing the great work and impact of a nonprofit organization. Often, stories are a way for the person telling them to heal and an empowering way for that person to give back and help others in a similar situation.

In an emotional story told on public radio station WBUR 90.9, thirty-year-old Lisa (last name withheld) spoke candidly about the drug use that destroyed her family and how a local nonprofit treatment program, Project COPE in Lynn, Massachusetts, saved her life and reunited her with her son.

Lisa said that she was motivated to share her story because she wants other mothers like her to seek treatment before it's too late. She also wants to break down the stigmas involved with addiction and raise awareness about the need for more funding for treatment programs like Project COPE.

stories from the real world

---

effectively share the stories, using both online and offline channels. An outside perspective may be required to help change the culture of the organization if it has never done this work before, or if staff is skeptical about the benefits of this approach.

When hiring a consultant to work with your organization, follow this to-do list to ensure that you are making the right decision:

1. *Do your research*. First things first—do your due diligence! Absolutely anyone can hang out a shingle and say they are a storytelling and/or social media consultant. Use online forums such as Quora, LinkedIn groups, and Twitter to research available consultants. Do you want someone local that you can meet in person? Do you prefer to work with a large agency or a solo freelancer? Do you care if the meetings are held virtually? Meetings and conference calls can be conducted via Google Hangout, Skype, and GoToMeeting if the consultant does not live in your area. Make a list of all the qualities you would like in a consultant, including location and experience. Do not go on price alone. Use this list when vetting potential candidates.

2. *Recognize what consultants do and don't do.* Storytelling consultants do not have silver-bullet answers or quick fixes to big-picture problems facing your organization. Most social media consultants do not work in an official capacity for Facebook, Twitter, or LinkedIn. We do not draw a paycheck each time someone signs up for a Tumblr account. I do not have a direct line to Mark Zuckerberg. (I sure wish I did!) My job as a storytelling and social media consultant is not to convince you to sign up on every social media platform, and it's not to tell you that sharing stories online will solve all of your problems. My job is to work with you to determine which platforms are right for you, based on multiple factors including staff capacity, technical knowledge, interest, fan base, target audience, and more.

3. *Go with your gut.* Just as in successful online community building and effective storytelling, a fruitful consulting engagement requires authenticity, trust, and complete transparency. If you get a bad feeling in that first meeting, go with your gut and try someone else.

4. *Come prepared with questions.* Consultants are very smart people, but we are not mind readers. If you say you understand, but you really have no idea what we are talking about, that is not going to benefit either of us.

5. *Be ready to do the work.* This is a BIG one. If you do not realistically have the time or the capacity to actually take action on recommendations and ideas provided by the consultant, then wait until you do before working with one. Working with a consultant should generate a ton of ideas and a long to-do list. Your storytelling and social media strategy don't have to start from scratch but may need to be reworked and improved. Be ready to jump in, or your money will be wasted.

Nonprofit consultants, just like personal trainers, provide practical tips for creating, implementing, and measuring a routine. Our work is designed to ensure that our clients can eventually go off happily by themselves to complete the plan we designed together. We are available to coach, motivate, and brainstorm along the way. If your organization is starting from scratch in this area, or if you have a plan that isn't working, it may be worthwhile to hire some outside help to point you in the right direction.

Challenge #2—Our Clients' Identities Need to Be Kept Confidential

This is a challenge I understand directly. As I've mentioned, I ran the development and marketing shop (i.e., me, myself, and I) at a small, community-based organization serving parents and children who had survived domestic and sexual violence. I understand the issue of confidentiality and safety well. In many cases, even if these families wanted to share their stories, their identities needed to be protected for their own safety and the safety of the staff. So we had to get creative when it came time for storytelling.

When working with a group where confidentiality is paramount, there are two things that you can do to get the story and a great visual without revealing the individual's identity:

◆ *Shield personal details.* Use a different name and identifying characteristics when describing the person. Make sure you are transparent when doing so. Include a footnote saying that some details have been changed to protect identities.

◆ *Use a creatively-staged photo.* The Plummer Home for Boys in Salem, Massachusetts is a nonprofit serving foster children. When it publishes a photo to accompany a story on social media, it stages the photo so that no one's face or identifying details can be seen. While showing the faces of the people served is very powerful, sharing a story with an imaginatively shot photo can also work well. In doing so, however, do *not* just conduct a web search and steal a stock photo image from another website. Your nonprofit will be at risk for copyright infringement and may be forced to pay a fine or succumb to legal action.

Some ways to gather stories in the face of confidentiality restrictions include:

◆ Speaking with alumni of the program—people who are not currently using services and who are not in immediate distress. Gather their success stories (or their on-the-road-to-success stories—maybe their story is still being told). The stories do not have to be 100 percent positive. There can (and very often will) be some obstacles along the way. At the domestic violence program where I worked, we contacted the women and children who had moved on from the program and were leading successful, healthy lives.

◆ Collecting stories from your donors as to why they give and from your volunteers as to why they volunteer. They all have stories of their own and a reason to be giving back to your organization. Most of them will welcome the opportunity to share their passion with others.

◆ Finding a local celebrity. At the program where I worked, we contacted a local news anchor who had lost a sister to domestic violence. She was willing to share her story at our annual breakfast. She spoke eloquently and emotionally about how she wished that her sister could have found a program like ours—how that may have saved her life. Invite a person who is well-known and respected in your community and who supports your cause to share a story or two with your audience.

Challenge #3—Our Clients Don't Want to Share Their Stories

To this statement, I say: Do not underestimate the people that you serve and do not assume they do not want to share their experiences! Empower them to share their stories.

I am positive that there are clients, volunteers, staff members, and others in your community that you have touched who are willing and able to share their stories. Current clients may be a no-go for safety or legal reasons, but take a look through your database of clients served, talk with program staff to get their recommendations, or conduct an anonymous survey.

If you still have serious trouble getting particular clients to come forward to share their stories, there may be a bigger problem at hand. Get to the root of the problem. There are many reasons why clients may feel reluctant to share their stories:

- ◆ They may feel exploited or distrustful. Perhaps a client or two shared their story with a staff member at your organization in the past, and they felt used or underappreciated. Ask them if they have shared their experiences before and what happened. Be sure to address any problems and challenges immediately.

- ◆ They may not want their experience with your organization to define them. I

> ### Animals Make Great Storytellers, Too
>
> If you do not work with human populations, collecting and telling emotional stories may seem difficult. But it shouldn't be! Animals often have wonderful stories to tell, as demonstrated by the Environmental Defense Fund (EDF) Polar Bear Odyssey email series.
>
> Throughout a six-part email series to prospective and current donors, EDF told the story of a fictional polar bear family as it struggled to survive amid the environmental changes in the Arctic. The campaign had every element that makes stories powerful—compelling characters, drama, a narrative arc, and a shocking conclusion with a call to action to support the work of the EDF as it works to save polar bears such as the ones featured in its email series.
>
> **Example**

remember that, at the domestic violence shelter, it was crucial for the survivors to hear that their experience with us is not the defining moment of their life. When asking for permission to share a deeply personal story, see what other information you can gather about the person. Ask questions about their hopes, dreams, and future plans.

◆ They may not be sure how sharing their story will directly help others. It is up to you to make this connection. Tell the client that breaking the silence and erasing the stigma around getting help will encourage others to step forward.

Sharing a personal story about a difficult time in your life is an emotional decision. Many people do not take that lightly. Make sure that the people you serve feel like they are giving back and helping to create change that will help others.

Challenge #4—My Nonprofit Is Too Small/Too New

There are many small nonprofits, even ones with only one staff member, who communicate very well with donors using stories. Sometimes the smallest nonprofits have the best stories to tell due to their size and proximity to supporters.

Choose one story to focus on and spread it everywhere you can. It may be the founder's story, it may be one success story, or it may be a story of starting out and needing assistance from the community to grow. In so doing, keep in mind that less is always more in storytelling and in social media. Your nonprofit, if it's very small or very new, actually has an advantage on the storytelling stage. You have fewer hoops and bureaucratic obstacles to overcome. Just try to create a compelling story about your staff or volunteers—how you are the new player in town, why your nonprofit was formed, and what you are planning to do next.

Challenge #5—We Don't Have a "Sexy" Cause

I hear this all the time, especially when it comes to social media and online marketing. "But, we don't have animals or kids to showcase! How can we possibly tell interesting stories and get them shared online?" Hold it right there. I am sure that there is a vital, important reason that your nonprofit exists. We can't all cure cancer, feed hungry children, and save endangered animals. There are significant needs in our society for the so-called "less-sexy" causes, be they community foundations, financial literacy organizations, historical societies, you name it.

Small and niche causes can sometimes have an advantage because their supporters are more dedicated and vocal. Use these supporters as your very own focus group to find out what messages and stories deeply resonate with them. What do they want to learn more about? What types of stories do they want to hear? Focusing on the dedicated supporters that you do have, rather than lamenting those that you don't have, is a much better and more effective approach to storytelling. Tell the stories your audience wants to hear, not the ones that you wish you had.

Challenge #6—My Nonprofit Is Worried about the Possible Negative Implications of Using Social Media

There is no doubt about it—social networking has changed the game regarding how people communicate, share information, and learn about new things in their lives. Nonprofits that do not embrace this tectonic shift in human communications will most assuredly get left behind. Despite the prevalence and popularity of social networking in our personal lives, using these channels for professional purposes can be a daunting proposition for nonprofits. Horror stories abound—staff members going "rogue" and posting inappropriate Facebook photos, volunteers tweeting too much information, and negative comments being

---

Getting Your Small or Niche Cause Online

An online and telephone survey conducted by the National Organization for Rare Disorders and Pew Research Center found that "[18] percent of [I]nternet users say they have gone online to find others who might have health concerns similar to theirs."

One survey participant, the mother of a young child suffering from a rare condition, wrote an essay about the lifeline of support that she found in an online community: "'When a disease is so rare, and there are no folks in your town, and few in your state who are going through what you are going through, you need a support group that encompasses people from all over the world. Getting to know people through the disorder has been an amazing experience and has created incredibly wonderful friendships and ties.'" Read more at *bit.ly/rare-condition*.

Nonprofits working to fund research for very rare diseases and other niche causes often have an advantage when sharing stories because the people they serve are actively looking for connections with others in their same situation. A small group of active, engaged, and passionate supporters is much more powerful than a larger group where the majority of people are more passive or even apathetic.

principle

---

left in LinkedIn groups. With all the fear mongering and bad news being reported on the incorrect use of social media and online tools, it is no wonder that nonprofits are wary of jumping into the social media pool.

For a nonprofit organization entrusted with the use of private funds, discretion, integrity, and trust are *everything*—one violation of this trust online could lead to loss of jobs, loss of funding, loss of community trust, or worse. While the fear of public indiscretions on social media is certainly understandable, it is also counterproductive. Simply put, the potential benefits of using social media to interact with current and prospective supporters vastly outweigh the potential negatives.

If you want to explore using social media for your nonprofit but are receiving pushback, there are several actions you can take to make the case to your colleagues and supervisors. Start by creating a clear and concise internal social media policy for all staff and volunteers. Before you jump into telling your stories on social media (even before you get a website or start an email newsletter), your nonprofit should have protocols and policies in place to empower and educate employees and volunteers on the use of online technologies. Make the consequences of violating these policies very clear. You may have policies regarding online behavior already in place but not readily enforced.

When developing a social media policy for the organization, answer the following questions:

◆ *What information should be confidential and why*? Is the safety of the staff and clients at stake if there is a confidentiality breach? Will you lose funding? Will you lose integrity and the trust of the community?

◆ *What do breaches of confidentiality look like*? Give specific examples, either made-up or from real life. Show offline and online examples.

◆ *What are the consequences of violating this policy?* What will happen to a staff person or volunteer? Unpaid leave? Denied access to posting and tweeting? Make sure that the degree of the consequence is reasonable and corresponds to the damage (or potential damage) that can or does result from a violation of the policy.

◆ *What behavior is encouraged*? Are staff and volunteers encouraged to share Facebook posts from the organization? Tweets? What resources are available to help them?

◆ *What behavior is discouraged*? What behavior is strictly prohibited? Are staff members prohibited from "friending" or "following" clients? What are the rules and guidelines around commenting as an employee of the nonprofit on blogs and social media platforms?

When policies are in place, conduct training for the staff and volunteers. Hold interactive seminars and workshops on social media tools and productive ways to use them. Your staff and volunteers already have social media accounts of some form or another. You can bet on that. Provide them with helpful guidelines as to what is acceptable to share online in a professional setting. This is a perfect teachable moment for younger people in the office who may not be accustomed to censoring themselves online in any way, and it will also create security for others who may not be sure where the boundary is. Social media training could cover topics like communications training and how all staff and volunteers represent the nonprofit (even on personal accounts); what is and is not appropriate to share on Facebook, LinkedIn, Twitter, personal blogs,

Get Those Legal Ducks in a Row

Since the social media space is still fairly new ground, many nonprofit organizations do not have formal internal and external policies guiding their staff and volunteer behavior as they navigate the online world. But due to the constantly changing nature of technology and the increasingly blurred lines between what is personal and what is professional, it is even more imperative that your organization be prepared and proactive.

Make sure that you solicit advice from a legal professional and a human resources expert when crafting your organization's digital and social media policies. Look up nonprofit social media policies online for examples and best practices. Do not be intimidated by this seemingly arduous process. In today's hyperconnected, always-on world, having policies in place and providing training and support in this area are necessary steps to protect your organization, your donors, your clients, and your staff.

watch out!

and the like; fundraising and promotion of the organization's events and mission; and the propriety of "check-ins" (think Facebook and Foursquare).

Show, don't tell, what a positive, productive social media presence looks like for your organization. In an interactive presentation, visually show your colleagues and supervisors what it would look like for your nonprofit to have a Facebook page—or a Twitter, Instagram, or Tumblr account. (You can always unpublish it or take it down later.) This will allow the board to see your nonprofit on social media for themselves and will make it more tangible.

Start small and grow from there. Do not attempt to be on more than two social networks at one time if you are just starting out and if your organization does not have a dedicated social media staff person. Begin with what you are most comfortable, so the learning curve won't be as drastic. Explain to your supervisor that you will regularly evaluate and measure what you are doing online (more on measurement and how to do it in **Chapter Thirteen**). Use a social media content calendar (more detail on this in **Chapter Eleven**) to demonstrate how you will do this thoughtfully and consistently, and stick to it. People who do not use social media in their personal lives may not see the value and may be fearful of what they do not know. Try to understand the causes of the skepticism you are facing and provide well thought out policies and information to combat it.

To Recap

◆ Even if your organization has never told stories before, there are several ways you can create a culture of storytelling and enthusiasm for sharing the stories on social media.

◆ Do not assume that the people you serve do not want to share their stories. Empower them and give them the tools to safely share their experiences.

◆ To deal with leadership and staff members who may be skeptical of social media, you need to show them evidence that it works for others and explain fully how you intend to use it.

◆ Create an internal social media policy and a plan for how the organization will manage its online and social media presence.

Part Three

Molding the Storytelling Gold: How to Promote Your Stories Using Your Website, Email, Blog, and Social Media

In this section, we discuss the best and most effective ways to utilize all of the online communications channels at your disposal—your website, blog, email, and social media—to share and promote your stories.

Chapter Eight

Your Nonprofit Website and Mobile Strategy

IN THIS CHAPTER

- ···→ The ten commandments of a great nonprofit website

- ···→ How to showcase your stories on your website

- ···→ What you need to include and feature on your Donate Now web page

- ···→ How to create and implement a mobile strategy

❝ Think of the story itself as gold. You mine the gold, capture the story. Then you bring it back to your office, and you need to pound that gold into different shapes and sizes depending on whom you're talking to, or also where you're telling it.❞

—Andy Goodman, a public interest communications consultant and speaker

In a book about *digital* storytelling, you may be wondering why the chapters delving into the actual, individual digital tools at your disposal are located in the last part of the book. This is to combat what I call the "tweet first" mentality. Nonprofits have a tendency to want to "tweet first"—that is, they jump on Twitter and start sending out tweets—without even knowing *why* they are using the platform in the first place. Or, in other cases, an organization may throw up a website without really thinking about how website visitors are going to engage with the site or even what it is they are supposed to do once they get there. Using digital tools without fully examining the "why" question is an invitation for confusion, frustration, and wasted time and resources.

My entire digital storytelling philosophy is built on this simple premise: It's not about the *tools*, it's about the *message*. It is my belief that you should spend the majority of your time learning about your supporters, crafting wonderful stories that will resonate with them, and creating actionable plans to disseminate these stories and connect with your audience. Only after you have a clear idea about the stories you are going to collect and tell, only after you know your audience inside and out, only after you have created a workable plan to move forward, then—and only then—should you dive into the shark-infested waters of social media.

Your Website Is Your Hub

You may be sick of hearing this by now, but it is so important, and it bears repeating (over and over again): Every single nonprofit organization, large and small, *must* have a website. Of course, I don't mean just *any* old website. Certainly not a static, never-changing, slapped-together, online brochure. Every nonprofit should aim to build a website that is their communications and fundraising hub—a strategically-designed, aesthetically-pleasing resource center that converts donors, recruits volunteers, and attracts new members to the cause.

Your nonprofit website is the most important fundraising and communications real estate you own. It is your most vital marketing asset. Your website is where the majority of people will go first to explore your organization and decide whether or not to invest their time or money in your mission.

So why are so many nonprofit websites neglected, clunky, and stale? If you want to be successful online, first and foremost, you need to adhere to my "Ten Commandments of Nonprofit Websites." How many does your organization follow—or break?

1. Thou Shalt Use a Content Management System (CMS)

A CMS is a website platform that easily allows you to make website changes and updates, publish a blog, and even more from one central page. No more expensive, hard-to-reach website developers and designers!

No matter which CMS platform you choose, there is no doubt that cumbersome, cluttered websites that require ivory-tower web experts to make even slight changes are the way of the past. Investing in a professional to design a fabulous looking website is one thing but paying an outsider to change one or two words on the home page (every single time you need to) is crazy and unnecessary. Fortunately, complete control and discretion in updating website content is now something that more and more nonprofits are demanding from their web designers and hosts. Take back your website power!

First Impressions Are Everything

You know you need a website but do you really know *why* it is so important for your nonprofit to have a great website? Without an easy-to-update, dynamic, visually appealing website, you will lose donors. Potential supporters are searching for your programs and services every day. You need a website in order to be found by people looking for you at the moment they are searching. Google (the #1 search engine in the world) prefers websites that are frequently updated, either via a news page or a blog (or both). You will make it easier for new and current donors to find you and to share your great work if you invest time and money into your website.

Also, without a website that houses photos, videos, and stories, you could lose your content. You own your website content. You do not own what you post on social media channels. While Facebook, Twitter, and other social media platforms are necessary and powerful tools to reach supporters, nonprofits cannot solely depend on them to get their messages across.

While connecting and engaging on social media is certainly a requirement of any nonprofit in today's digital age (see **Chapters Eleven** and **Twelve**), the reality remains that each channel directly controls what users see and when they see it. Any of the major social media platforms could alter themselves completely at any time with no explanation required. If your nonprofit has built up an audience solely through Facebook or Twitter and these channels make changes to their terms of service or even shut down completely, you have no recourse and your posted content will be lost. This is why I recommend optimizing your nonprofit website first—where you have the most control and where you own the rights to your content—and then using social media to drive supporters there to get more in-depth information, read and view longer stories, and make a donation.

My favorite CMS is WordPress. A close runner-up is the increasingly popular Squarespace. Both have blog capabilities and can be completely customized with your nonprofit's branding, logo, and colors. (CMS platforms frequently change in response to the latest online trends so make sure to do your due diligence before choosing one for your organization.)

There are many advantages of having an easy-to-use, inexpensive CMS including customizable themes and blog embedding. Most themes on WordPress and Squarespace are free (and we know how nonprofits love things that are free). Some do cost money but are well worth it, and all themes can be customized by graphic designers and web developers if you so choose. A good CMS platform will also have the ability to incorporate your nonprofit blog into the website. Blogging is vital to your digital marketing strategy and needs to be on your website, not hosted somewhere else. (Don't have a blog? Just wait for the next chapter.)

If you do need to redesign your website, find a web developer that works with WordPress, Squarespace, or another CMS platform that you prefer. Get the training necessary to maintain the site yourself. In fact, get training for a few key staff members, so it is not left to just one person—namely, you.

The actual brand of CMS is not important (and I have only listed two out of dozens available), but whichever you choose, it must be easy for a nontechnical person to update and be accessible via mobile devices.

2. Thou Shalt Write for the Web

Repeat after me: "I will not cut and paste language from our grant proposals into the website. I will not cut and paste language from our grant proposals into the website."

Writing for the web is very different from writing for print audiences. (And entirely different from writing a formal grant proposal!) Good and effective writing for the web is short, sweet, and to the point. It should be succinct. Write one or two sentence paragraphs with one idea per paragraph. The paragraphs should be limited to one hundred words or fewer. Less is always more. The text of the paragraphs should include bulleted lists, subheadings, and bolded headlines. Be sure not to ramble or use passive language. And avoid clichés, fluff, and jargon.

3. Thou Shalt Use Professional Graphics and Photos

With the rise of visually-driven social media sites like Pinterest and Instagram, the entire online space is increasingly focused on eye-catching visuals.

Creating your own graphics with Adobe Photoshop or online tools such as Canva or PicMonkey is great for social media and blog posts, but the DIY spirit does not suffice when it comes to your website. You have approximately two seconds to capture website visitors' attention before they click away to the next thing. It often takes a professional designer and photographer to capture this attention.

Your nonprofit website needs to feature the following visuals:

◆ Strong photos. Can the photos featured on your home page convey your mission and impact in one or two seconds?

◆ Professional graphic design. This includes a consistent, branded look for the website, blog, all social media sites, and email newsletter.

◆ Social media icons on the bottom of each page. I suggest leaving social media icons at the bottom of each page so they are easy to find but do not take away from the website content. When people visit your website, the goal should not be to entice them to leave it to visit Facebook or Twitter. Social media buttons should be visible on your home page for those who want to connect with you there, but they should not be the most prominent images on your site.

4. Thou Shalt Incorporate Consistent, Simple Navigation and Design

In my experience and opinion, a comprehensive nonprofit website should have no more than ten sections (less is always more). You should be able to tell your stories, entice involvement, and describe your mission and programs in ten or fewer sections. See what can be consolidated. See what can be eliminated entirely. I am sure that you can cut out more than you may initially think. Be brutal in your editing! Gone are the days when a potential donor or volunteer is going to spend twenty minutes (or even five) looking around your site. If they can't find what they are looking for immediately, they will leave.

The ideal nonprofit website is easy to navigate, consistent in layout, and pleasing to the eye. That means you should use the same font and color scheme throughout the site. All pages should be the same dimensions (one or two columns), and all photos should have the same dimensions and placement on the page. There should also be a search function that allows your visitors to quickly and easily navigate to the information they are seeking.

5. *Thou Shalt Feature Impact Stories Prominently on Your Website*

In this book, we have talked a lot about the power of stories in helping you achieve your nonprofit's goals. If one of those goals is raising money (and I'm willing to bet it is), then you need to feature your best, most compelling stories on your website.

Think of the many reasons why people make donations. Most people give from the heart based on an emotional response, not from a sense of logic or rationale. They may also give rather impulsively. Your nonprofit needs to get into the minds of your supporters and feature the right stories on your website. If helpful, go back to **Chapter Four**, where we discussed the six types of stories you need to be collecting. Focus on impact stories for your website.

The upper portion of the home page should feature a large, clear image of a person or persons that have benefited in some way from your services. That photo should instantly tell your website visitors a small story about your mission and what it is that you are working to achieve. A potential supporter should be immediately drawn in and wanting to learn more. Your nonprofit story should

---

Creating a Collection of Images and Photographs

Start a digital library of photos and graphics that you have explicit permission to use. Keep them in cloud-based storage like Dropbox, Box, or Google Drive. Mark them as "Permission to Use" and make sure to give attribution to the photographer where required and keep a database or folder of written copyright permissions.

Avoid purchasing cheesy, overused stock photos that you find online. You want your website to feature moments and snapshots of the people that you serve, the services that you provide, and the impact that you achieve. The photos need to be specific to your organization and your cause. Be sure that you have permission to use the photos of your clients and of any other people in the photos.

Never steal images from other websites or blogs. Do not go to Google Images and download the images you find there. If you are discovered, legal action could be taken and your organization could be held monetarily liable for the misappropriation of the images. For more places to get reputable images, visit Beth Kanter's frequently updated "The Ultimate List of Free or Low-Cost Image Collections" at *bit.ly/Kanterlist*.

 practical tip

be woven through each page of the website from the "about" section to the contact page. Think about using stories to entice people to get involved rather than just a laundry list of ways to help.

Housing a diverse selection of impact stories in a particular, dedicated section of your website is also a great idea. Nonprofits that do a fantastic job of collecting and showcasing impact stories on their website include the Harlem Children's Zone (*hcz.org*), Denver Rescue Mission (*denverrescuemission.org*), and Women for Women International (*womenforwomen.org*).

Remember: Your website exists to educate people about your mission, but it also exists to inspire them to take action on behalf of that mission. Otherwise, why have a website at all? The best way to do this is through compelling visuals and succinct storytelling, threaded throughout the site.

6. Thou Shalt Have a Clear Goal

You managed to get some visitors to your website, and you have shared your powerful stories with them. They are inspired and motivated to help you accomplish your mission and to be part of writing a happy ending for those you serve. So what do you want your website visitors to do next? Donate? Volunteer? Sign a petition? Subscribe to email updates?

In reality, it is very rare that first-time, uninitiated visitors to your website are going to make a financial donation. They may be arriving on your site from Facebook, Twitter, a Google search, or any number of online channels. You may want to direct website visitors to your email newsletter sign-up so they can stay in touch and keep informed of your great work. You may want them to sign a petition, thus capturing their email address for further advocacy appeals.

Of course, if you are designing a large, multichannel fundraising campaign, you will want to feature a large, colorful "Donate" button on the home page. It all depends on your goals, what has worked in the past, and what you estimate will give you the biggest bang for your buck in the future.

Just like charity: water, your nonprofit's CTA should be featured prominently in the top half of your website with a compelling graphic or image accompanying it to make it stand out. It should be absurdly easy to find what I'm looking for with one glance and to figure out what you want me to do with another.

If you want me to attend an event, make that a prominent button on the home page with great photos of the people who will be helped from this event. If you want me to volunteer, include a great photo of your volunteers, a positive quote or story, and an easy way to sign up.

7. Thou Shalt Have a Super-awesome "Donate Now" Landing Page

I am of the camp that clickable buttons online should take you exactly where you want to go. If the shiny online button says "Give Now," do not take me to a page where I can "Learn More" or "Get Involved." I clicked on that button to give! Don't be shy about taking me there. The "Give Now" button should link *directly* to the online donation form where I can enter my credit card information and press "Submit."

Creating Brand Ambassadors

When you first enter charity: water's website, you do not see an appeal to donate money. You see a colorful, eye-catching video all about water, asking visitors to set up a social fundraising campaign. (Visit *charitywater.org*.)

By making a prominent CTA on its home page, charity: water is encouraging its aspiring supporters to spread the word about its mission on social networks. These brand ambassadors will raise awareness and eventually funds to help the cause.

This approach works. Prominent celebrities and online influencers have set up charity: water campaigns and raised millions through social media campaigns. They donate on their birthdays or to honor anniversaries and special events and are able to raise much more money than if they had only written a check themselves.

 stories from the real world

Whether or not you think this is tacky, the fact remains that a large, prominently placed "Donate" or "Give Now" button has been proven to increase online donations. Studies have also shown that, for some reason, a green Donate button outperforms a red one. However, regardless of the color you choose, one with color outperforms a black or gray button every time. Make sure your colorful Donate button is visible from each page of the website.

Use video and feature your best impact story on your donate page. Google conducted a survey and found that telling a story via video is an incredibly powerful tool on a nonprofit's website, with 57 percent of people saying that they made an online donation after watching a charity's video!

Eliminate all obstacles to getting that online donation when they are on your donate page. It may seem obvious, but in the dozens of nonprofit donation forms I have filled out in my life, I have yet to see the KISS rule in practice. (I like to say that the rule of KISS means "Keep It Simple Silly"—mainly because I always tell my seven-year-old daughter never to use the word stupid.)

You need to understand that you are not entitled to anyone's money (or attention for that matter). The more time I need to invest into filling out your form heightens the chance that I may get distracted and click away before I am finished. If your nonprofit has a tedious donation process, it will ensure that many potential donors will leave you high and dry.

Feeling a sense of security when giving money online is paramount. Make sure you are accepting online donations through a recognized online giving platform or using Square, Apple Pay, Google Wallet, or any other easily recognized payment vendor. Also, place the appropriate verification and security badges on your donation page and include a disclaimer that the credit card information is not stored by your nonprofit.

Another tip to get increased donations is to offer suggested giving levels and monthly giving options on the donate page. Make it easy for people to give year-round! Offering monthly giving options on a website has been shown to result in bigger, longer-term donations. This donation page from North Shore Elder Services in Danvers, Massachusetts offers several options and a button to click to make it a monthly recurring donation: *bit. ly/NSESdonate*. Similarly, my local NPR affiliate station, WBUR, makes it very easy to contribute monthly with its easy-to-complete online donation form: *bit.ly/WBURdonate*.

Personally, I tend to give more to a charity when I can spread it out over twelve months rather than providing a huge lump sum at the end of the year when my budget is often stretched thin due to the holiday season. Encourage your donors to think that for the price of a latté, they can be doing something good once per month.

Once you receive an online donation, encourage your supporter to share the good deed! This donor just gave money and contributed to a cause about which the donor is passionate and feels great about the gift—and what it will accomplish! This is the ideal time to ask your donor to share their passion for your organization on the donor's social networks. A pop-up message or a "Thank You For Your Donation" landing page with social share buttons will do the double duty of getting your organization in front of the donor's friends and family and offering social proof—"Hey, my cool friend, Julia, trusts this organization. I should check it out!"

It is also vital to automate the process to make sure online donations are acknowledged immediately. People are used to instant gratification after online purchases and expect the same from the nonprofits they support. Sending an email hours after the fact or (the horror!) a letter in the mail are not sufficient in the digital age. Embed a vibrant, enthusiastic "Thank-You" message to pop up immediately after the donor has submitted the donation. For extra points, make it a "Thank-You" video! (And don't forget to ask your donor to share it on social media!)

8. Thou Shalt Capture Emails

Most email software companies (iContact, Constant Contact, MailChimp) have an easy-to-insert "Email Sign-Up" button and graphics designed for your website. Keep in mind that asking a website visitor for an email address is a very intimate request in today's world of spam, email overload, and digital overwhelm.

Be creative when asking people to give you their email address. I suggest moving away from the traditional, dull

Get People Inspired to Fundraise for You

More charities are including a "Start a Fundraiser" option on their donate pages to give donors more options in their philanthropic activities. The logic behind this method is: "I may only be able to give $25 to a cause, but if I am especially passionate about it, I can start my own online fundraising page and ask my friends, family, and social networking connections to participate and give." Peer-to-peer giving, as this is commonly known, is one of the most effective ways to raise money as people are much more likely to give to a person that they directly know and trust.

Barbells for Boobs is a nonprofit dedicated to the early detection of breast cancer. On its simple, uncluttered donate page, it encourages visitors to take one of three actions: Join its "Lifeline" of donors who provide monthly recurring donations, give one gift today, or create a personal fundraising page. Every action is clear, concise, easy to understand, and most importantly, easy to complete in just a few clicks. Setting up a personal fundraising page, which can then be shared via social media and email, can be completed just by filling out a short registration form. You can see its donate page at *barbellsforboobs.org/lifeline*.

practical tip

language, "Sign up for our email newsletter." We all receive way too many of those on a daily basis. Consider wording the request to explain how it connects to your mission: "Join us now to save the oceans," or "Keep up with the many ways you can help save children from hunger."

Of course, you have to provide compelling content in your email newsletter to get people to *stay* subscribed. More on effective nonprofit email marketing in **Chapter Ten.**

9. *Thou Shalt Have Much White Space*

Please! Just because you can fill the screen does not mean that you should.

The ideal nonprofit website is heavy with large, colorful images and light on text blocks. It has bullets, bolded headers, short paragraphs, and a lot of links. It also has a lot of white space to make the site clean, professional looking, and aesthetically pleasing.

10. *Thou Shalt Be Mobile-friendly*

As previously discussed, your nonprofit website is the hub of all your marketing and fundraising operations. It is your most important and vital marketing real estate. It is where the majority of potential supporters will first come to find out more about you, sign up for your email list, experience your impact, and eventually, make a donation.

If your site is not mobile-friendly, it could be penalized and not appear high up in Google search results (and with recent changes to the way Google determines the order of these results, non-mobile-friendly sites are being pushed down). This means that if potential supporters or clients in need are searching for you using a phone or tablet, they may not be able to find you easily. Not being found online at the exact time someone is looking for your programs and services will result in lost revenue and missed opportunities.

Getting Started with a Mobile Strategy

Despite the proliferation of mobile devices among all demographics, too many nonprofits think that having a successful mobile strategy means just creating a website that can be read on smartphones. In reality, an effective mobile strategy encompasses design, content, and messaging into all channels used for marketing and fundraising—websites, emails, appeals, and events, as well as blogs and social media.

Having a "mobile strategy" does not just mean ensuring that your website looks okay on mobile devices. Rather, a great mobile strategy ensures that your supporters are getting and processing your information on their mobile devices. Success on mobile means that your readers can do everything they need to do to interact and engage with your nonprofit— easily and without obstacles—while on their smartphones.

Implementing a mobile strategy is now a must for nonprofits. According to comScore, the number of mobile-only adult Internet users surpassed desktop-only Internet users in March 2015. That means that more of your supporters are visiting your website from a mobile device than from their desktop computer! This extreme shift of Internet use to mobile devices has enormous implications for the nonprofit world with respect to fundraising and constituent communications, as the competition for resources is fierce and donors' attention spans are shrinking.

Recent studies have found that more than half of all emails sent are opened initially on a mobile device. Durham+Company found that nearly one out of five donors has made a gift using a smartphone or tablet—an increase of 80 percent from 2013. While online giving is still a fraction of total giving, it is the segment that consistently grows the fastest year after year.

Pew Internet has also reported that an increasing number of young adults, African-American and Latino adults, and low-income adults rely on their mobile devices rather than desktops or laptops for online access. Nonprofits that work with these populations need to pay attention to the portion that is "mobile only" and design their communications accordingly.

There are several ways to start creating and implementing an effective mobile strategy for your nonprofit. The first step is to get out your copywriting and editing hats. Each piece of marketing and fundraising content you produce needs to be unique, persuasive, clear, concise, heavily visual, and easily digestible. (Whew!)

The types of content most read and shared on mobile devices are valuable blog posts and articles, shareable links, key updates, photos, and videos. Remember the readers and how they consume news, email, and social media updates. If they are using their smartphone or tablet, they are most likely using it while doing something else like waiting in line at the grocery store, or attending their child's soccer game, or watching TV. Get creative about ways that you can capture their attention while competing with numerous distractions.

Remember that less is always more on a mobile device. Allow plenty of white space between the body of your text and CTAs and prioritize short paragraphs and bulleted lists to make your content easier to read. Also, do not make the text too small to read on a mobile device (no smaller than size 12 font). Make the links easy to tap or click on with a finger.

The most effective way to encourage readers to click on links is to feature large, colorful buttons embedded into the content. However, make sure that the clickable button or image is named properly in case the image is stripped out of the email and the reader only sees text in its place. For example, Gmail accounts automatically strip out images from emails until the user approves images from that particular sender. This is done to prevent spam and viruses from entering your in-box, but it can also

---

The Google Mobile-friendly Website Test

Google, the #1 search engine in the world, has decided that its users are tired of searching for things on their mobile devices only to be brought to a website that doesn't load or is not accessible. Its own research found that over 50 percent of all Google searches occur on smartphones, tablets, or other mobile devices. Based on this research and feedback from its users, Google now scans the web and displays search results based in large part on how well a website can be navigated on a mobile device.

This all means that, if your website is not mobile-friendly, it will now be penalized in mobile search results. Google knows that if a site is hard to read with tiny text and lots of clutter, its users will click away, looking for something else. This is particularly the case for younger people and millennials. Younger generations are driving the age of mobile, and they have very high expectations and low attention thresholds. You don't want to miss out on these donors and volunteers. You want to get them involved early and keep them engaged for the long haul.

The good news is that you can test your website using Google's free mobile-friendly test: *google.com/webmasters/tools/mobile-friendly*. Websites are ranked either mobile-friendly or not. There are no varying degrees. So make sure to take the Google mobile-friendly test and to talk to your web developer about mobile-friendly options for your site—or risk getting left behind.

important

be a difficult hurdle for email marketers looking to create aesthetically-pleasing email newsletters.

Speaking of aesthetically-pleasing email newsletters, they need to be completely overhauled. Long, three-column, graphics-heavy emails simply do not work as well in our mobile-obsessed culture, where bite-sized content like short videos and Internet memes rule. More email is now read on mobile devices than on desktop computers or laptops. The old-school nonprofit email newsletter should now function more like email blasts—short, to the point, and with a clear call to action in the middle. (The next chapter on email marketing goes into more detail on this topic.)

Use a single column template for your email blasts to supporters and donors. Do everything you can to prevent the text and photos from overlapping. You do not want your readers to have to pinch the screen on their phones, scroll, or zoom in too much. Rather, add more detailed information on a mobile-friendly website or blog post and have readers click on a link in the email to access it.

Notably, nonprofits should not be spending the money and resources on creating a distinct, separate mobile website. You should have one website that functions as the complete and total information hub of your organization. This way, all the information is in one place, and it is less cumbersome to update than two sites, one mobile-friendly and one not.

Consider a "responsive design" template for your website. Responsive web design is a method of creating websites designed to be accessed and viewed across a wide range of devices and screen sizes. With responsive design, you ensure that no matter what device your supporters use to find you, the website will adapt to the screen size. Most platforms including WordPress and Squarespace are automatically responsive. If you are working with a website developer, be sure this service is offered.

Always think of your potential website visitors first. What are they looking for on your website? How are they finding it? I am sure that for some of them, being able to access your site information from their smartphone and their tablet—with ease and efficiency—is a priority.

Think like a newspaper editor and reflect on the "hook" of any type of content you produce. Always be asking: How can I word this story headline to grab people's attention and make them read more? What can I call this video to entice people to watch it? Blog headlines and email subject lines are more crucial than ever in the era of mobile news and information where you have a split second to capture someone's attention and get them to read more. Most people who check their email from their mobile device only see the first forty-five characters of a subject line (depending on the device) so put the good stuff up front, keep it short, and make it timely and relevant.

Using photos, videos, colorful graphics, and other visuals is the single most important way to cut through the clutter on mobile devices. Where possible, make all images clickable links to send readers to more information, to sign up for an event, to donate, or to otherwise act on your CTA. Keep in mind that while you want to be visual, you do not want to stuff too many images and graphics into your content that can overwhelm it. So be sure to think strategically and thoughtfully about which bright, colorful, and eye-catching photos can help convey your impact in an instant. One photo, or a photo collage, is often stronger than a long series of multiple images. Think carefully about what will catch your readers' attention and draw mobile users to your website.

My biggest piece of advice is this: Do not purchase a mobile app for your organization. Focus on optimizing your website, email newsletter, and all marketing and fundraising content for mobile first before delving into the world of mobile apps. I warn against nonprofits building their own individual apps for their organizations because the majority of smartphone users only download and use apps for gaming and social media or to get a value-added service (finding the cheapest gas, finding coupons, or receiving loyalty rewards). If your supporters aren't going to use your app on a daily basis (and if it doesn't provide an immediate value or service to them), they won't even bother downloading it.

It is also rare that an agency, company, or organization designs an app that is widely used when the browser on the mobile device works just as well to find information (if not better in some cases). Mobile apps are expensive and complicated to design, develop, and promote. Ask yourself what you could accomplish with a stand-alone app that you couldn't accomplish with a well-executed mobile strategy.

To Recap

◆ Great nonprofit websites are easy to update and easy to navigate, and they focus on the desired action they want visitors to take when they get there.

◆ Impact stories need to be prominently featured on your nonprofit website through photos, videos, and your blog.

◆ The optimal nonprofit website donation page features a compelling impact story, provides a simple and secure way to enter payment information, and offers opportunities to share with social networks.

◆ Always make sure you are reaching your audiences *where they are*, not where you want them to be. And where they are is on their phones, tablets, and other mobile devices.

Chapter Nine

Storytelling Through Your Nonprofit Blog

IN THIS CHAPTER

···→ Benefits of blogging for nonprofits

···→ How to create a blogging plan

···→ How to think of topics about which to blog

···→ Maintaining your blog once it's up and running

D espite the surging popularity of social networking platforms including "micro-blogging" sites like Tumblr and Twitter, traditional long-form blogging remains one of the most important weapons in any storytelling arsenal. Not only are well-written blog posts effective for visual storytelling, but blogs also remain incredibly popular across all age groups. Online publishers Fractl and BuzzFeed analyzed how several different generations consumed online media and discovered that from millennials to boomers, blogs rank as the most popular type of content on the web.

The word "blog" (short for "web log") carries certain connotations, as many people still think of blogs as the realm of crafty moms, travel journalists, and people with something to get off their chest. However, the larger, more established nonprofit organizations were early adopters of the blog, reaping the many benefits of increased website traffic, email sign-ups, and online donations. A high-quality, interesting, unique blog has been shown to have a direct benefit on website traffic and fundraising.

So why do so many nonprofits ignore this powerful storytelling tool? And more specifically, how can smaller and less tech-savvy nonprofits get on board with blogging to create a dynamic outlet that shares their stories, grows their support base, and helps them accomplish their goals?

Does the World Really Need One More Blog?

You may think that the Internet is completely saturated with bloggers and there cannot possibly be room for one more. I disagree. All you need to start a blog is a passion for the topic and a real interest in sharing stories and experiences related to that topic. If what you write is relevant to a particular audience of people, then there is a need for it.

The blogosphere is full of people sharing their ideas and, yes, there is a lot of noise and clutter out there. However, there is *always* room for a well-written, thought-provoking, and entertaining blog. Hopefully, that's where you come in!

Why Have a Blog For My Nonprofit?

A blog is the best place to share your best stories and showcase your impact! Your blog is an online tool that you own and that you control. Facebook will undoubtedly change its algorithm (again), Twitter could be sold to a third party and change its terms of service, Instagram's popularity could dissolve. But the content you produce and publish on a blog is yours forever.

A blog will also help in the following ways:

- ◆ Improving your SEO, which means you are more likely to be found when someone is searching for you or for organizations like yours

- ◆ Building trust and community by helping to establish your nonprofit as an authority on a particular issue

- ◆ Bolstering the content on your social media channels

- ◆ Driving website traffic and increasing email sign-ups

- ◆ Compelling people to make a donation when they are on your website

- ◆ Perhaps more importantly, telling stories on your blog will continually force you to examine two tough, but vital, questions:

  - ❖ *What impact are we having on the world*?

  - ❖ *What would happen if we disappeared tomorrow*?

Where Do I Start?

As with any marketing strategy, you need a measurable goal to determine success. Starting a blog is not a marketing strategy in and of itself. Rather, it's a tool just like storytelling. You need to know where you are and where you want to go before you begin. Start by asking: What is the goal for our blog? Do you want it to establish authority, build trust, showcase impact, increase website traffic, grow your email list, help you advocate for a particular cause, and/or raise awareness?

Write down three big-picture goals for your blog. These goals need to tie directly into your nonprofit's marketing and fundraising objectives, which we identified in **Chapter Three.** When writing down goals for the blog, always be thinking about the measurement of success. How will you know if your efforts have been successful? (Lucky for you, measurement and benchmarks are covered in more detail in **Chapter Thirteen**!)

Afterward, ask yourself the following:

◆ How will you be held accountable for these goals?

◆ How will these goals be measured?

◆ How often will you run reports and review them? Monthly? Weekly?

After you have set some concrete goals for your nonprofit blog and determined how you can measure success, it will be easier to get approval from executive staff and board members. If you assure higher-ups that you will be accountable for the blog's progress and that you will ensure that the time spent is helping achieve the overall marketing and fundraising goals for the nonprofit, they will be much more likely to get on board.

What's Next?

Tell staff, board members, volunteers, and VIP donors about your blog first. Be excited! Get the storytelling and social media committee involved. Let them know that you are going to call on them to help you find content and to promote the blog. Consider holding a special meeting to announce the start of the blog. (You may need to educate some staff members on the importance of having a blog and to dispel the notion that it's not just "one more thing to add to the pile.") Use this blog launch meeting to solicit ideas for blog posts. Remember that all ideas are welcome.

In managing your blog posts, create a blog editorial calendar—either in Google Calendar or in a document in Dropbox that can be accessed from multiple places. This will help you keep track of ideas for stories and photos for the blog and how often they should be developed and posted. A blog editorial calendar template can be found in.

What Will We Write About?

Many people mistakenly think that the only time-consuming aspect of blogging is in the actual writing of posts. Given the multitude of tasks that maintaining

---

Using Your Blog Editorial Calendar

A blog editorial calendar is essential to help you plan a wide variety of blog posts and sync with the important happenings at your nonprofit. In creating your calendar, take a look at all the events and important dates through the year. Match the blog post and the story you are telling to the time of year. For example, the start of school, holidays, Mother's Day, a special cause awareness day, a fundraiser, and the like.

Your blog editorial calendar should include the following:

◆ Post date – When do you aim to post the article?

◆ Author or authors responsible

◆ Working title (or at least a descriptive idea for the content)

◆ Status – Is it being researched? Do you still need a quote or a photo to go with it?

◆ Category – What is the broader topic covered in this post?

◆ Tags – What are some more specific topics, people, places, or organizations covered in the post? More on tags later in this chapter.

◆ Keywords – Think strategically about keywords and how people will be searching online to find your post

◆ Call to action – What is the specific and measurable action you want people to take after reading the blog post?

◆ Notes

a blog entails, it is no surprise that multiple people should be tasked with managing the creation and posting of blog content. Indeed, there are four equally important tasks to be undertaken when maintaining a successful nonprofit blog: research, writing, formatting and editing, and promotion.

Research

Research is essential to whittle down the list of topics about which you will eventually write. I suggest doing a huge brainstorming session for topics. Make sure to include stories prominently on this list (See **Chapter Five** for ideas on finding great stories.) When brainstorming, always remember that you want to be a resource for your readers. A place they look forward to visiting and to which they will direct their friends and colleagues. Proper and thorough research will lead to stories that fulfill this goal and promote your cause in the variety of ways in which you seek support.

We know that our stories are our most impactful type of content. Other than continually sharing stories in our blog posts, what else can we write about? Here are some suggestions for other kinds of nonprofit blog post topics:

Frequently Asked Questions

Every nonprofit has a list of frequently asked questions (FAQs). Take a look at your organization's FAQs section if it is on the website. If you don't have one, brainstorm FAQs with a group and write them down. About what issues do you get the most emails and phone calls? What are people repeatedly asking you on Facebook, Twitter, and LinkedIn? Compose a list of the top ten FAQs for your organization. Each answer can turn into a blog post. Add a short video to the post for a more interesting visitor experience.

Myths vs. Facts

What are some of the myths, misconceptions, and stereotypes surrounding your organization, your cause, or the people that you serve? Think of the top five myths that you regularly encounter in your job and use your blog as the opportunity to dispel some of those myths. Consider adding links to other blog posts and articles that support evidence dispelling these myths. Linking to reputable outside sources helps to create community and makes your blog more authoritative, authentic, and credible.

Video Testimonials

Videos can be collected from donors, clients, staff, volunteers, or community members. An effective video can be long form and made with a professional film company, or it can be informal, short, and filmed with a smartphone. Videos can be easily embedded into blog posts. Add a brief description to the video and violà—instant blog post! We will discuss more ways that your nonprofit can use video in storytelling in **Chapter Twelve.**

Newsjacking

If you have not done so already, sign up for Google Alerts. Google Alerts is a free service that sends you a daily or weekly email featuring all the latest news on topics of your choosing. Sign up to get a Google Alert for your cause, for example, "domestic violence," "wetlands preservation," or "animal abuse."

In tying current news stories to your blog, ask yourself: What is happening right now in the world or in your community that is relevant and timely? How is it of interest to your audience? Why is everyone talking about it? This method of adding to a trending, topical discussion is often called "newsjacking."

How to do it: Choose a news story from a reputable outlet and write two to three paragraphs commenting on the issue on your blog. Describe why the news story is important, what the implications are for your cause, and what it adds to the overall discussion. Then post a link back to the news story for your readers to "Read More." Encourage your readers to join the discussion with you in the comments section of your blog.

You may be able to plan ahead to use these kinds of news stories on your blog, but you also need to be flexible and adapt to the news cycle and what's on people's minds. A good mix of topical, relevant, and timely posts around current events and issues, along with planned blog posts, is ideal.

How-to Posts

Do people come to you with questions about taking action? Do your supporters want to participate, but are confused about where to begin? In your blog, you can create a "how-to" post to identify actions supporters can take to benefit your organization and the community it serves and to aid them in taking those actions.

Some ideas for how-to posts could include a step-by-step list for collecting food for a food drive, ten tips for raising money when you are participating in a fundraising walk, five ways to prevent elder abuse, or seven things to know when calling a legislator.

Blogs Done Right

There are many examples of interesting, well-written nonprofit blogs. What they all have in common is that they consider their audience first and they provide value in the form of stories (sharing impact), resources (providing value) or, in the best cases, both.

Here are some of my favorite nonprofit blog posts for your inspiration:

◆ Trees for the Future features stories from the field, usually written by the executive director, with a lot of great photos. (*treesforthefuture.org*)

◆ Nothing But Nets showcases the important work it does, written in the context of the global fight against malaria. (*nothingbutnets.net*)

◆ The ASPCA features a Pet of the Week and a lot of feel-good stories from pet owners. It also provides updates on its legislative impact, which is of great importance to its donors. (*aspca.org*)

◆ The blog posts of TWLOHA (To Write Love on Her Arms) are very diverse, written by a variety of people suffering from addiction, anxiety, grief, and/or depression. TWLOHA aims to reach and help more people through the stories it shares. (*twloha.com*)

◆ The Nature Conservancy blog is a fun, helpful resource where Nature Conservancy scientists, science writers, and external experts "discuss and debate how conservation can meet the challenges of a nine billion+ planet." (*blog.nature.org/science*)

◆ The tagline for the Ronald McDonald House Charities blog is, "A glimpse into the lives of Ronald McDonald House Charities volunteers, supporters, staff, and families." Though the subject matter and content varies, all of the bloggers have something in common—they have all been touched by Ronald McDonald House. (*ourrmhblog.wordpress.com*)

◆ Global Exchange Reality Tours focuses on reflections and testimonials from the participants of its "Reality Tours." (*globalexchange.org/blogs/realitytours*)

◆ The Darkness to Light blog provides advice for parents on ways to minimize opportunities for abuse of children and teens. Particularly useful are testimonials from parents and guidance on how to talk to your kids about difficult issues. (*d2lblog.com/category/our-perspective*)

Example

Think about how your organization can benefit from people answering a CTA. Create a list of three topics on which you can offer advice to your supporters, providing them with ways you would like them to take action and detailed instructions on how to do so. And, as an added bonus, you can feature a story of a person who took this action, how it was done, and what impact it had!

Top-ten Lists

Everyone loves top-ten posts! The post does not even have to contain ten items. Any number will work as long as it's in list format. In creating the list, always think of what will be useful and helpful to your online community.

Examples include Top Ten Dog Training Tips, Top Ten Tips to Keep Kids Active in Summer, Top Ten Tips for Saving the Environment.

An excellent way to get a lot of engagement and shares on a top-ten list is to create an accompanying infographic with a free tool, such as Infogram, Venngage, or Piktochart.

Infographics

Speaking of infographics, they are everywhere and increasing in popularity! According to a fabulous interactive infographic from Neomam (*neomam. com/interactive/13reasons*), our brains crave infographics because we suffer from information overload. Information presented in a visual and colorful format is 80 percent more engaging and about 323 percent more accessible. Internet searches on infographics have grown over 800 percent in the last year alone!

Find infographics online to use in your blog if you cannot create your own. Search Pinterest or Google for your cause plus the word "infographic" or use the Infographiqs search engine. (*infographiqs.com*)

For example, enter the words "environment infographic" or "hunger infographic" into your favorite Internet search engine or social media site. When you find a great infographic that relates to your mission, locate the "embed" code on the infographic. The "embed" code is used to insert the graphic on your blog with a direct link back to the original source and can usually be found at the bottom of the web page where the infographic is located. Note that, if there are no embed instructions, you will need to ask the creator's permission to share the infographic on your blog. Once the infographic is embedded into your blog post, write one or two paragraphs summing up the most interesting and thought-provoking highlights of the infographic. Make sure to always give credit where credit is due and to link back to the original source!

Examples of great nonprofit infographics can be found on my Pinterest board at *bit.ly/NPInfographics*.

Writing

Now that you've done your research and you have a list of possible blog topics, you need to actually sit down and write the posts. Easier said than done! When writing, it is important to remember that you are writing for your audience. They are unique. Don't forget to be focused on your community and not your own agenda when creating a blog post. Furthermore, as we have previously discussed, your audience is not "everyone with a pulse." It is better to have fifty passionate blog readers than five thousand blog subscribers who barely pay attention. Use the blog as an opportunity to tell your story and authentically connect with your audience.

At the outset of my writing efforts, I find it helpful to do a "brain dump" and put everything down on the page, and then sort it out later. You can

---

Evergreen Content vs. Timely Content

When creating the blog editorial calendar, you want to ensure a good mix of evergreen and timely content.

Evergreen blog posts are those with content that remains relevant long after it is written. The principles and theories that are presented will not get dated. These posts can indeed be updated and revised over time, but the basic structure and message will remain the same. An example of an evergreen post could be, "Ten Things to Avoid Saying to Someone Who Has Cancer" or "Five Ways to Prevent Elder Abuse in Your Community."

While evergreen blog posts are vital to incorporate into your nonprofit's blog, your audience will also want posts that are about current events and issues relevant to your mission. They will want to get information on the present state of affairs at your organization, your up-to-the-minute impact, and ways they can get involved. An example of a timely post could be, "The Time Is Now to Call Your Senator about Fracking" or "Seven Ways You Can Help Survivors of Hurricane Sandy."

principle

also use voice-capturing software or your smartphone to dictate parts of the post. After this brain dump, create an outline and a structure for the post. Think of the stories that you have collected and how they can be incorporated into the post. Not every blog post will involve traditional storytelling, but it should have a clear beginning, an opening paragraph carefully worded to grab the reader's attention, a middle section with the "meat," or substance, of the post, and a conclusion, summing up the main points and incorporating your CTA. Remember, a blog post can be between three hundred and five hundred words and contain a photo or video. It does not need to be the next great American novel. That said, longer-form blog posts have been shown to perform better in Google searches. Mix it up between long posts and short and see which get the most traction and engagement from readers.

Only when you are done writing should you choose a headline. Make it catchy! The headline is the most important part of the post. Make sure it will fit in a tweet or the subject line of an email and that it is compelling enough to entice people to click on it. For inspiration, look at other blog headlines that grab your attention. Place yourself in the shoes—and minds—of your audience and determine, in this frantic, busy world, what headlines and blog titles would cause you to click to learn more?

Formatting and Editing

The look and feel of a blog post are incredibly important. There needs to be an eye-catching visual (or more, depending on the post). Paragraphs should be one or two sentences only. Avoid large, unbroken blocks of text. Use bolded headlines and bulleted lists to highlight important points and break up the text.

Use Visuals

It bears repeating that when formatting your blog post, it is important to include a good visual of some kind. According to a study by HubSpot, blog posts with photos receive 53 percent more likes and attract 104 percent more comments than those without. You can create your own graphics with free online tools such as Canva, or search photo sites such as Getty Images and Flickr Creative Commons for photos you can use. (Make sure that you are reading the fine print when choosing a photo that is not yours, so as not to run into any legal and copyright issues.) If your blog only has text (and big, unbroken blocks of text, at that), it makes it that much harder to share, to pin, and to tweet. Images are key. It's a visual world, so get on board!

Select Categories and Tags

Categories are overall topics that describe what the post is about and help your readers find other posts like it. On the other hand, tags are more specific and get into more detail. For example, say you have a recipe blog and you want to write a post about brownies. The categories you would use would be "Dessert" or "Baking" and tags would be "Chocolate," "Brownies," and/or "Walnuts." Setting up categories and tags from the very beginning will enable your readers to easily find posts on topics of interest.

Choosing the Right Platform

WordPress and Squarespace are not just my preferred CMS options for nonprofits, they also win the award for my favorite nonprofit blog platforms due to their affordability and ease of use. This arena, however, is ever-changing, so do your research and see what platforms other organizations are using.

There are many benefits of using a CMS such as WordPress and Squarespace for your blogging platform. Both WordPress and Squarespace are already optimized for search engines and for mobile devices, saving you a lot of time and headache. You do not need to know HTML or website coding to start, as they offer a variety of "drag and drop" templates from which to choose. They can be managed easily from your desktop or mobile device, and you can authorize multiple users, authors, and editors to access the blog.

In addition to their other great features, both platforms offer a huge variety of "plug-ins" that will make your life easier, from automatically sharing a new blog post on social media channels when published to automatically blocking and deleting spam comments. Plug-ins work like little pieces of software designed to enhance the functionality of your blog platform. Most are free, though some require you to pay a nominal fee.

My favorite WordPress plug-ins are Disqus Comment System, Akismet, WordPress SEO by Yoast, Jetpack, CommentLuv, and WordPress Popular Posts. For a complete directory of WordPress plug-ins and their individual uses, go to *wordpress.org/plugins*.

practical
tip

Enable Comments

Enabling comments on your blog encourages two-way communication with your readers. In my opinion, why have a blog if the comments feature is disabled? What is the point? I'm not sure, but I see this all the time. Rather, you want to actively encourage your online community members to interact with your blog and to add their thoughts and opinions. This creates trust and helps you build a loyal readership.

Another pet peeve of mine is blog comment sections that are clearly unmonitored. If left untended, they fill up with spam. Spam comments are like weeds in a garden. They can kill a vibrant blog if not deactivated! Monitor the comment section of your blog daily and get a spam-preventing plug-in to help limit or eliminate potential spam.

Promotion

If you write it, they will come! Well, not necessarily. All wildly successful bloggers say that you need to spend as much time on blog promotion as you do on creating new content. Sometimes even more!

Here are a few ways to increase your blog readership:

◆ Add social media share buttons to each post. When I come across a blog post that I really enjoy but there are no social media share buttons anywhere to be found, I get frustrated. See, I want to share your wisdom with my friends either via Facebook, LinkedIn, or Twitter but I want it to be as easy as possible. Your reader (i.e., me) is busy. I do not want to have to cut and paste links and search around to find the Twitter button. Put the social media share buttons prominently under or on the side of *each* blog post to make it easy to spread your good works.

◆ Post the blog link to all social media channels where you are active. I suggest going onto each individual channel and posting the link to make sure that it looks professional. Blasting out your blog post link to every social media channel automatically upon publication looks unprofessional and unpolished.

◆ Inquire about syndication of your blog posts in your local or regional newspaper. Contact the publishers of each to find out the requirements for syndication. Often local papers are hungry for original content, and they may be willing to run your blog posts in the Op-Ed section or community section.

◆ Create a blog promotion checklist and refer to it after you publish each post.

Julia's Blog Promotion Checklist

After a blog post is published, I share the link to several social media sites:

☐ Facebook page

☐ Twitter

☐ LinkedIn - personal profile, company page, and relevant LinkedIn groups

☐ Google+

☐ Pinterest

☐ Tumblr

☐ StumbleUpon

☐ Reddit

☐ Digg

☐ Delicious

☐ SocialMarker.com

☐ SocialAdr.com

☐ Scoop.it

☐ NetSquared

☐ Quora

I take the time to craft a message to accompany the link, taking into account character limits and the audience on each social media channel. For a better reading experience, I make sure that the thumbnail (the preview that people see before they click on the article link) includes a great visual.

◆ Feature a snippet of the blog post in your email blasts, always including a link back to the original post on your website.

◆ Ensure that interested readers can subscribe to your blog to see a new post when it's published, either via email or RSS feed.

◆ Don't be passive when promoting the blog post! Ask board members, staff, and volunteers to share the blog posts (within your established social media policies, of course). Read them at staff meetings and encourage comments. Make it a team affair. Remember, you cannot do it alone!

I often receive this question about blogging: "Should we cut and paste our blog content onto other sites, such as LinkedIn, Publisher, and Medium?" The answer is not a simple yes or no. There are pros and cons to sharing your original blog post content on several different sites. Many hugely successful bloggers say that it is okay and even beneficial to republish an original post on other sites as long as you wait two weeks after the initial publication. This is to avoid Google indexing your posts as "duplicate content" and therefore penalizing you in search results. If you do decide to republish your original post on different sites, I suggest a slightly different headline for each platform.

Getting People to Share Your Blog Posts

The Customer Insight Group at the *New York Times* published a study exploring why people share content online. It found that people share to bring valuable and entertaining content to others, define themselves to others, grow and nourish relationships, give self-fulfillment, and market causes or brands. How can you help your community accomplish these things through your blog? Spend some time and dedicate some resources to creating content that is well-written, original, compelling, timely, relevant, and interesting. This may seem like a tall order, but that's what it takes to stand out in the noise of the Internet.

Keeping up Momentum

According to HubSpot's State of Inbound 2015 report, most marketers spend one to two hours on a five-hundred-word post. It's a lot of work to be successful! Try not to get discouraged if your blog readership grows very slowly. Not everyone will be a superstar blogger. Blogging is more like a marathon than a sprint.

Work with influencers who can get you more blog traffic but make sure they are interested in your cause. Just because someone has fifty thousand Twitter followers does not mean that your cause will resonate with the influencer or, for that matter, the influencer's followers. Actively look *everywhere* for people who are passionate about your cause. Ask them to share your blog posts and to submit ideas or stories for future articles.

To Recap

- There is no doubt that having a well-written, well-read blog is a lot of work. Time and resources need to be invested in doing it effectively.

- The four major tasks involved in maintaining a successful blog are research, writing, formatting and editing, and promotion.

- Stories should be the hallmark of your nonprofit blog but consider also writing posts that help, educate, and inform the audience about your cause and issue.

- When looking for blog post topics, think of ways you can dispel the myths, misconceptions, and stereotypes encountered by your organization and the people that you benefit.

- A hallmark of success for a great nonprofit blog is creating and maintaining a passionate community of readers, not the sheer number hits on the post or traffic to the page.

Chapter Ten

Creating Great Nonprofit Emails That Inspire Action

IN THIS CHAPTER

···→ Nonprofits need to change up their traditional email newsletters

···→ Ten steps to more effective nonprofit emails

···→ How to use email to share powerful stories

···→ How to grow your nonprofit email list

At least once per week, I get the question, "Is email dead?" And I always answer, "If you think email is dead, then you are definitely using it wrong." The truth remains that, love it or hate it, email is still one of the best ways to connect with your supporters. Email is used by almost all age groups and demographics (tweens and teenagers may be the exception), and it is accessible via a wide range of devices.

Social media and mobile marketing may be trendy, but study after study show that email remains consistently ranked as the best online tool with which to raise money. The 2015 M+R Benchmarks Study, a nonprofit industry standard for reporting on online advocacy and fundraising, found that for every one thousand fundraising messages delivered, nonprofits raised $44. Sixty-seven percent of nonprofits surveyed for the 2016 Nonprofit Communications Trends Report stated that email is their most important communication channel. Connecting with your donors and constituents in their email in-box still works but it's all about doing it the right way.

In this chapter, we will cover the characteristics of nonprofit emails that get opened and read, the importance of incorporating stories into your email communications, and best practices in the sector that you can use to build up your subscriber list.

Let's Stop Using the Word "Newsletter"

I want to clarify that I loathe and detest the word "newsletter." "Newsletter" implies something long, wordy, full of jargon, and not very exciting. Ironically, when I think of nonprofit newsletters, I do not think of news. I envision an organization dumping information that it believes is relevant and timely but often is the exact opposite. I prefer "ebulletin" or "eblast" because it implies something brief, urgent, and important.

Your Emails Shouldn't Be about You

As with all other communication tools that we discuss in this book, my number one tip for activating supporters is to make your message all about *them*. The platform with which you choose to communicate with constituents is not as important as the story you tell them on it. And the best

---

How Often Should I Send Emails?

The answer? More often than you think.

I recommend sending shorter emails more frequently. One client with which I worked sent an incredibly long email newsletter once per quarter. That means it communicated via email with its donors only *four times per year!* Can you imagine if the donors deleted even just two of those emails? That's 50 percent of its communications for that year! No wonder its donor attrition rates were high and new donor acquisitions were so low. People had completely forgotten about it!

Nonprofits need to reevaluate how they are using email lists. Too often, nonprofits think that sending out an email means asking for money. Are you using your email list like an ATM? This is not a very effective strategy since you will get deleted, ignored, and unsubscribed. Sending brief, interesting email updates frequently to your donors on the great work you are doing as it happens is a much better use of your time and your donors' attention.

 practical tip

way to set yourself apart from all the competition in your donors' email in-boxes is to provide useful and valuable information.

Make Your Emails Count

Too many nonprofits use email and social media as a way to only push out event notifications, fundraising appeals, and other requests. Nonprofits need to reframe their thinking, especially when using email. It helps to picture an actual human, passionate about your cause, sitting down and reading your email. Will this email inspire this person to take action? Or will the person pass it by or (heavens no!) click the delete or unsubscribe button?

How to Tell Stories with Email

You have outstanding programs to promote, events to advertise, and corporate sponsors to acknowledge. But if you only have two seconds to grab the attention of a supporter, will you squander it by sharing the minutes from your last board retreat?

The most well-designed and beautiful email newsletter in the world will not get read or shared if the content it provides is not valuable to its readers. Think back to **Part One** and the work you did around identifying your target audience members and their pressure points. Your email subscribers gave you something precious—permission to communicate with them via their overcrowded in-box. After years of being overwhelmed with sales emails and spam, this is not something we give to people lightly.

Donors, supporters, volunteers, and email subscribers all have one thing in common: They want your nonprofit to demonstrate that you are accomplishing your mission and that you are a worthwhile cause to support. This support can be in the form of their attention (in the beginning), their time, and then, hopefully, their money.

This is the part where those fantastic stories about your impact come in. Stories are the best way to prove that you are making a difference in a brief, compelling, and easy-to-digest way. And using email to disseminate these stories is one of the best ways to raise funds for your organization.

Remember that you use email as part of your online communications toolbox to keep your organization on top of the minds of your subscribers. That way, when the moment is right, they will take action on your behalf. The more your email subscribers learn about you, your impact, the people served, and the lives changed, the more connected they will feel. If they feel connected to you and if they trust you, they will be more receptive to giving, sharing, and volunteering when asked.

Stories, Stories, Everywhere!

Twenty places to find stories and other content for your email communications are:

◆ Program directors

◆ Front-line staff (administrative, office support)

◆ Thank-you notes received

◆ Annual report

◆ Old print newsletters

◆ Annual appeal letters

◆ Organization files and archives

◆ Grant proposals

◆ Press releases

◆ Volunteer orientation materials

◆ Presentations you have given

◆ Google Alerts or another research tool

◆ Your community partners

◆ Your competitors

◆ Donors, foundation funders, corporate sponsors

◆ Community events

◆ Community news

◆ Blog posts

◆ Prestigious and trusted sources from around the web

◆ Volunteer profiles

The basic principles of fundraising still apply when using email: It's all about the message you convey and the relationship you build, not the tool you use to do it!

Creating More Effective Nonprofit Emails

Now that you have a collection of great stories to share with your email subscribers, what are some steps you can take to ensure that your emails get opened, read, and acted upon?

It is your job to make sure you have permission to send to each email address that you enter into your list. It may seem like a no-brainer but it is extremely bad form and possibly illegal to automatically add people to your email list if they have not given you explicit permission to do so. Do not add your family members, friends, and every business card contact that you receive to your nonprofit email list. Subscribing to email updates is a much more intimate way to connect to a cause than a casual Facebook like or Twitter follow. You must respect this relationship and show courtesy to your dedicated email subscribers by not adding people who have no desire to be there.

To avoid any legal issues and to help ensure you have permission to send your emails to the addresses on your list/listserve make sure you use a hosted email marketing service. These services, such as MailChimp, iContact, and Constant Contact, to name only a few, are relatively cheap or free for nonprofits, are easy to use, and, best of all, help ensure that you do not run afoul of CAN-SPAM (Controlling the Assault of Non-Solicited Pornography and Marketing Act) laws. (To make sure that your email marketing and fundraising campaigns are complying with the law, go to *bit.ly/ftc-email-law*.) In addition, they provide nifty templates for your emails, automatically manage all unsubscribes and new subscribers, and provide detailed statistics on each email you send out. (More on the importance of these statistics later in this chapter.)

When creating email communications to subscribers, be able to express a good reason to hit the send button. What makes this email in-box-worthy? Sending on the first and the fifteenth of the month like clockwork may seem like a great idea, but your subscribers always need a good reason to hear from you.

A "good reason" to send an email does *not* automatically equal fundraising! Yes, you should be using email strategically to fundraise and to cultivate donors. However, if the only time your email list members hear from you is when you need money, they are going to tune out and hit the delete or unsubscribe buttons. Some "good reasons" to send an email, other than asking for money, include:

◆ Wanting to share helpful resources with your subscribers

◆ Acknowledging and thanking a special donor or volunteer

◆ Sharing a great story about a person you have served or the work that you are doing

◆ Bringing attention to an issue of importance to your subscribers

Only communicating with subscribers when there is a relevant reason will also demonstrate that you are not abusing the privilege they have granted you and will improve your nonprofit's trust and credibility.

How Can I Tell If My Emails Are Working?

Are your emails getting you the results that you want? This all goes back to the SMART objectives you created in **Part One.** Each email communication should fit into your objectives, insofar as you are using it to get more supporters to your website, readers to your blog, and/or online donations. Remember that sending out emails is a tactic and the software itself is a tool, not a goal or an objective in and of itself.

If you are using email software like Constant Contact or MailChimp, you can access a detailed report after the email is sent out, telling you how many people opened the email and what they clicked on. However, do not get caught up in mere "open" rates. While important to keep an eye on, open rates often do not mean anything at all regarding accomplishing your objectives. I often open emails by accident only to delete them one second later, not having read them at all.

A better metric of success is to discover what your readers clicked on after they opened the email. Did they click on the link to your latest blog post? Did they click on the "Donate Now" button? Did they click over to a petition you included and sign it? Armed with this information, go back to your goals and your SMART objectives to determine if your email campaigns are helping you make progress.

 practical tip

Research has shown that emails sent under a person's name rather than an organization's name have higher open rates. This makes sense because humans naturally want to connect with other humans. Just like on social media, people much prefer to connect with a name and a face rather than a brand or a logo. Experiment with creating emails from the CEO with the CEO's photo and contact information at the end. Change it up every once in a while and have the email sent from other people in your organization—volunteers, clients, staff. Of course, the person does not have to actually write the email. You just need to get permission to use the person's photo and name as the sender.

Work hard to make sure the email is about the subscriber. Start your email with the words "thanks to you" or "because of you" and go on to tell a great story about the impact subscriber helped your organization achieve. Even if a subscriber is not yet a financial donor, the attention and support have made a difference. Make the email subscriber the hero of the story and provide encouragement to continue the great work by getting further involved and helping write the ending to the story.

In the digital age where we are accustomed to communicating in 140 characters or less and via text message, your email subscribers are definitely used to a more casual tone. Using humor works well in an email if thoughtfully done. Try being friendly and upbeat in your email. However, if you are sending an email about a serious issue, make sure the voice you use in the email matches the subject. It may take a few attempts to find your true nonprofit voice, but do what comes naturally and what best fits your nonprofit's personality.

Pew Internet reported that the majority of emails are now being opened on a mobile device. Nonprofits have less and less space in which to capture a readers' attention. Remember, when crafting an email campaign, ask yourself: What do you want readers to do once they have read your email? What story are you telling in your email? If you are sharing a profile on a volunteer, ask the readers to click on a link to sign up to volunteer or to spread the word to others who may be looking for an opportunity. The CTA must make sense in the context of the email and the CTA should not always be "Donate Now!" Not only that, you should also aim to write email updates that are so wonderful that your readers will share them with others! Help them out by making it incredibly easy for them to do so by adding social media share buttons at the top or bottom of the email. Place a link at the bottom of each email that says, "Share this email with your friends. They'll thank you." You can also create a web link to the email that can be shared on your own social networks.

How to Build Your Email List

If you can give people a good reason to give you their email address, they will. It's a little more challenging for nonprofits because we cannot offer coupons, discount codes, or other tangible incentives in exchange for an email address. However, we can offer trust, authenticity, and credibility.

A Word on Subject Lines

Take some time when crafting the email subject line. There is no doubt that the subject line is one of the most important pieces of the email puzzle. As with a headline in a newspaper, the words you choose are vital in enticing the reader to open the email and read more.

Do not call it "November Email Newsletter" or "Newsletter Issue 4." Instead, give a peek into the stories and content you are sharing. For example, if you are providing resources on local summer activities for kids to keep them away from TV and screens, the subject line could read, "Tips to Keep Kids Active in Summer." If you are sharing a success story about a client, the subject line could read, "Kira Was about to Give Up— Then This Happened." Consider the difference between an email with the subject line, "Polar Bear Population Rapidly Decreasing," and one that asks, "Do You Want to Live in a World Without Polar Bears?"

How long should your email subject line be? Marketing company Return Path conducted research on almost ten million emails from businesses and nonprofits of all sizes. In its report entitled, "The Art and Science of Effective Subject Lines," it found that there is no relation between the length of the subject line and the number of emails opened/read and that 25 percent of email subject lines are forty-one to fifty characters. Interestingly, subject lines with sixty-one to seventy characters had the highest read rate of any email (17 percent). Keep in mind that a typical desktop email client shows about sixty characters of an email subject line. The proliferation of smartphones and tablets have changed the email game dramatically by only displaying twenty-five to fifty characters depending on the size of the device. Keep these character counts in mind when crafting your email subject line.

practical
tip

We can also offer a promise to never spam our list, to always send valuable information, to only send emails that are necessary to send, and to never sell our email list. Here are some tips to grow an engaged email list:

Ask for Email Addresses Everywhere You Communicate

This includes a sign-up form on your website, on social media sites, at events, in your print newsletter, in your annual report, in all annual appeals, and more.

Say "Join Us" or "Stay Informed"

Change the language that you use from "Sign up to receive our newsletter" to "Stay informed," "Help the cause," or "Get exclusive stories and news first!" Email newsletters and blasts are so ubiquitous now that people often ignore them, delete them, and unsubscribe without even giving it a second thought. To entice your supporters to join your email list (and stay on it!), you must make it sound fun and exciting and, above all, worth their while.

Make It Secure and Easy

If you have a very long email subscription form to fill out with twenty required fields, people will be much less likely to complete it. Ask for a first name (to personalize the emails) and an email address. If you need to ask for more information, try to limit it to four items. The more obstacles you put in people's way, the more they'll click away from your sign-up form and go on to something else without completing the sign-up. Assure people that their email address is secure with you by using a recognized email hosting service and letting them know they can unsubscribe instantly at any time.

Promote Exclusivity

Your email subscribers should get your best stuff! Share an inside story or photos from a CEO's recent trip out in the field before sharing it on social media. Invite them to a special Q&A session with the board president available only to email subscribers. Give them unique glimpses into the inner workings of your organization.

Beware of Contests

Be careful of holding a contest or sweepstakes solely to collect more email addresses. Growing your email list for the sake of growing it is not the goal. For the same reason you would not want ten thousand fake Facebook fans, you do not want people on your email list who are not interested in your mission or passionate about the cause. If you hold a contest that makes sense in the context of your mission, you will attract like-minded potential supporters. However, if you hold a sweepstakes and give away an iPad, you will attract everyone who just wants an iPad, not the people who will become dedicated, passionate advocates for your nonprofit.

Be Interesting

Think of the important adage of "WIIFM"—What's In It For Me? What can you offer them via your email? Emails that contain unique insight into your programs, a feel-good story about a client, or a special heartfelt thank-you from the CEO will all encourage your email subscribers to stay engaged.

To Recap

◆ The goal of all email communications is to entice people to open them and take action based on what's inside.

◆ Send emails out regularly and only to those who have explicitly given you permission to do so.

◆ The most important tip on effective emails for nonprofits is to know your audience members well and give them what they actually want (not what you think they want).

◆ Be sure to review the detailed metrics report about your email after it is sent out. That way, you can go back to your goals and your SMART objectives to determine if your email campaigns are helping you make progress.

◆ With the majority of emails now being opened on mobile devices, your email subject line needs to be clear, concise, and compelling.

◆ Offer exclusivity, valuable information, and compelling stories to potential subscribers to grow your email list.

Chapter Eleven

How to Use Social Media to Tell Your Story

IN THIS CHAPTER

···➔ The three basic principles of social media success

···➔ Julia's Nonprofit Social Media Checklist

···➔ How often to post

···➔ How to get more engagement

The "tweet first" mentality is easy to understand. Social media continuously receives an overwhelming amount of media and press coverage and no nonprofit wants to miss out on the next big, new thing in marketing and fundraising. Stories abound about nonprofits using social media to raise tons of money (ALS #IceBucketChallenge, anyone?) and advocating for social change such as the marriage equality movement. Individuals, brands, and nonprofits are all scrambling to keep up with the latest tips and tricks on using these social channels to engage with their digitally-connected constituency.

There is no doubt that social media is an incredibly powerful tool in the digital age. However, it is important to note that it is just that—a tool. It is the people connected and the relationships built with these tools that make them effective for marketing your cause and fundraising for support.

As we know, using social media platforms by themselves is not a very effective marketing or fundraising strategy. However, when used in conjunction with other online marketing tools such as your website (see **Chapter Eight**), blog (see **Chapter Nine**), and email campaigns (see **Chapter Ten**), social media can help spread your message to new supporters. Indeed, all of these channels should be working together, like a well-oiled machine, to help you deepen your connection with current donors and to expose your great work to new ones.

What Is "Social Media"?

The term "social media" refers to online tools that allow people to share information, create photos and videos, and exchange ideas via online networks and communities. Some of the most widely known social media sites are Facebook, Twitter, YouTube, and LinkedIn.

Social media sites and apps are highly interactive and fluid. Email newsletters and websites are not generally considered social media since they are methods of one-way communication and discussions do not occur on the platforms themselves. The exception to this is blogs, which can be very social and interactive in the comments section.

If just reading the words "social media" gives you anxiety, I am here to assure you that you are not alone. Working in this industry for several years with clients large and small has shown me that nonprofit professionals tend to be very uncomfortable and lack confidence in their abilities to use social media on behalf of their organizations.

People all over the world use social media every single day to share photos, experiences, news stories, and cat videos. They use these tools to become better informed, to be entertained, and to learn more about the people and causes about which they care most. Love it or hate it, social media tools have completely revolutionized the way in which human beings communicate, interact, and consume information. Nonprofits need to understand social media and not be afraid of it or write it off as a trend.

The Basic Principles of Social Media

This chapter is not going to focus on the technical uses of each hot social media *tool du jour*; these tools and platforms change so frequently that a new one will most certainly crop up by the time you finish this sentence. However, as with traditional fundraising, the principles of success on social media translate across platforms and are pretty much incontrovertible.

The formula for success on social media is actually very simple: Deliver value when, where, and how your audience wants it. Of course, this is much easier said than done. Where I've found most nonprofits need help is coming up with creative and efficient ways to deliver this desired value and to measure the results of their efforts. This is what we will cover in these next three chapters.

Start by finding out what your audience values. By audience, I mean the people that you are trying to reach when using social media platforms.

To Pay or Not to Pay—That Is the Question

When social media first came into the conversation and became a major player the digital space, it seemed like signing up was a no-brainer. Sites like Facebook, Twitter, Instagram, LinkedIn—all the big players—let businesses and organizations register accounts and post to their fans and followers for free. Nonprofits set up shop, started building their audiences, and posted happily for a few years. In today's cluttered environment, with one-sixth of the human population on Facebook alone, it is getting next to impossible to have most of your posts seen by your fans and followers. This is where spending a little bit of money to promote your message on social media comes into play.

Should your nonprofit pay for ads on social media? My short answer is yes. There are several benefits of advertising using social media platforms that set it apart from other forms of traditional advertising. You can target the people who will see the ad based on their interests, demographics, and much more. You can specify the budget for the ad. Most of the time just $10 makes a big difference! Another benefit of social media advertising is the measurement of results. With a TV or billboard ad, you never know who has seen it and what action they took in response to it, if any. With social media ads, you can measure clicks, views, and other actions taken in real time, as the ad is running, and make tweaks and improvements along the way.

The benefits of spending money on social media ads are many, but you need to be strategic in the implementation. Before jumping in, consider the reasons behind creating and promoting an ad on social media. Be strategic in the audience that you target with your ad. Be sure it incorporates eye-catching visuals in the form of a great photo or video as well as catchy language designed to get people to take the desired action. As a sector, we need to eliminate the outdated concept of social media as free and easy. Nonprofits should become comfortable with spending money (and time) on these tools to adequately compete for donors' attention in the social media space.

(This was discussed at length in **Chapter Three,** defining key audiences for your digital storytelling efforts.) Talk to them. They are people after all! Ask them in person and via email. Use social media to listen to your audience members and to conduct research about their preferences and their passions and then continue the dialog that they have begun. Only by giving your audience members what they want, where they want it, and when they want it, can you succeed in the social media jungle.

The basic principles of social media are as follows:

◆ Social media is a tool, just as the telephone is a tool. Simply hooking up a phone in your office is not going to make the donations roll in.

◆ You have to earn the right to ask for something on social media, just like asking a friend for a favor. You wouldn't ask someone that you just met to help you raise a thousand dollars (at least, I hope you wouldn't!). Social media also works in this way. You need to get to know the channel, the context, and the community before jumping in and promoting your agenda.

◆ Quality versus quantity, always. Despite your first impressions on the topic, social media is not a popularity contest. Yes, it may make you feel good to have ten thousand Twitter followers. But if only a tiny fraction of those followers actually care about your organization, what is that community worth to you?

◆ Similarly, there is no silver-bullet solution and no magic key that will unlock thousands of new, passionate followers or online donors. It takes consistent effort and creativity to make your mark.

◆ There is also no "one-size-fits-all" solution. Success on social media looks different for every organization. UNICEF has very different goals than the local dog adoption agency down the street.

The Three D's of Social Media Success

That being said, I have found that there are three things that, when done well and when done together, often promote success for organizations jumping into the social media pool. I call them the "three Ds." They are diversification, dedication, and dynamic content.

Diversification

Have you heard the term "multichannel marketing" or "diversification of channels"? These are fancy ways of telling you not to put all your marketing and fundraising "eggs" into one online "basket."

Diversification requires thinking outside your own comfort zone. Be where your supporters and your donors are, not just where you want them to be. If your supporters are using a social media platform you have never heard of, get in the game. Experiment. Take webinars and read blogs. Get on that site and start using it. It doesn't matter that you dislike Twitter or don't understand Snapchat. What is important is that your donors and supporters love and understand these channels—and you need to, also!

Most importantly, do not just rely on the old methods that have "always worked" for your nonprofit. Trust me, your donors are smarter and more tech-savvy than you think. Just because they enjoy getting a paper annual report does not mean that they are not active on Facebook. (In fact, many of them would probably enjoy the monetary savings of getting that paper report in the form of an online infographic that they can easily share with their social networks!)

It is important to note that I am not recommending replacing tried-and-true methods of communication with social media. If your donors love to get phone calls from you (and I am sure that they do) or if they love their print newsletter, then, by all means, keep at it! Diversification only means that you should explore a variety of additional channels of communication and get the word out about your organization, its mission, and its good work for the community in as many places as possible. It means not being limited by assumptions about your donors and a fear of new things.

Dedication

As a passionate nonprofit professional, you are undoubtedly being pulled in a million directions. There is a shiny new social media tool coming out every single day (sometimes, every hour). The sheer amount of information and resources available can be overwhelming.

You have my express permission to stop, turn off the computer, turn off your phone, and breathe. Do not rush to try out every flashy new app or social media platform that appears (even if your board president suggests it). Start out slowly, thoughtfully, and with purpose. Consistency and quality win the social media race every time.

By the same token, don't give up on a social network because it's not doing exactly what you want it to do immediately. Be patient. Your followers need some time to figure you out, to build trust and affinity, and to start liking your posts and your tweets. And you need time to figure out the specific language of the platform, the audience, the etiquette, and the strategies that work best. Social media is a marathon, not a sprint. (However, if you find that, after giving it your best shot, your supporters are not using a particular channel or not engaging at all, regroup and evaluate. See the next chapter on measuring the success of social media efforts.)

Dynamic Content

There is no substitute for what I like to call "dynamic content." Dynamic content, for purposes of digital storytelling, is creating posts, tweets, photos, and videos that make your fans and followers love you, engage with you, and share your organization with their networks. This is the only way to survive the brutal social media jungle and cut through the everyday noise and clutter. The term "content" refers to anything that you create and share widely such as social media posts, tweets, blogs, videos, photos, infographics, white papers, ebooks, annual reports, appeal letters, email news, and more.

Dynamic content is so good, so funny, so informative, and so invigorating that your followers can't help but share it. Dynamic

---

The Danger of Tasking an Inexperienced Young Intern to "Do Social Media" for Your Nonprofit

Using social media tools is not a skill that is intrinsic to young people simply because they are of the "right" generation. No one is born knowing how to use these tools. As tempting as it is, I warn my clients all the time against thinking, "Let's have the nineteen-year-old intern handle it; he's on Instagram all the time!"

It takes time and effort to develop the skills necessary to do the work of social media correctly. It takes strategic planning, thoughtful brainstorming, and consistent posting as well as a willingness to receive criticism and feedback (not all positive). Using Facebook in your personal life is very different from strategically using Facebook to further the goals of your nonprofit. Be thoughtful about who is placed in charge of social media content development and postings. Consider tasking more than one person with creating and making these posts. This will help ensure that posts remain fresh, thought-provoking, and relevant.

watch out!

content provides value to an audience. It is helpful, useful, valuable, and entertaining. These are no easy feats, but they come with the territory. You need to invest some time in content creation for your nonprofit. Your stories are an integral part of the dynamic content you create. They are the best part. Stories provide the meat for all of the posts and tweets, and stories are what entice others to share. To ensure a dynamic mix of great content including photos, videos, articles, blog posts, and more, use the social media content calendar template provided in.

Nonprofits using social media not only have to compete with businesses, brands, and other nonprofits for the attention of their supporters but they also have to compete with a user's friends, coworkers, and family members! That is a tall order, but I believe that even the tiniest nonprofit can use great content to raise its profile, find new supporters, advocate for a cause, and promote events. The possibilities are only limited by creativity and resourcefulness.

FAQs

Five of the most frequently asked questions I receive regarding the use of social media for nonprofits are as follows:

Which Social Media Platforms Should My Nonprofit Be Using?

You should always be using the platforms your *supporters* are using. To find out which platforms they are using, you need to do some good, old-fashioned market research.

Start by conducting research within several of the most popular social media platforms to see if and where people are discussing your cause and your organization. If you are a national nonprofit, look at national trends in social media use by generation and income level and match that to your donor database.

For smaller nonprofits, survey your donors, board members, staff, volunteers, clients, and other people connected to your organization to find out which platforms are most relevant to them.

Do not assume just because most of your donors are "older" that they are not using social media. In fact, the baby boomer generation is the fastest growing demographic buying smartphones and the fastest growing generation signing up on social media networks. In fact, a common complaint I hear is that nonprofits have trouble finding "younger donors."

Well, guess where these younger donors are? On their phones and on social networks! So get in the game before you get left in the dust.

Once you have compiled a list of prospective social networks to explore, write down the pros and cons of each network. If you do not understand the platform or if you need help understanding, you need to do some homework. Listen to webinars, talk to other nonprofit professionals who are active on those platforms, and attend educational events and seminars to get you up to speed. A major "con" would be failing to understand how to use the network in the first place!

Think of each social media channel as its own country. You want to visit Turkey, but you have no experience with the language, culture, or etiquette. To have the most productive trip, you need to do your due diligence and

---

No, You Are Not Posting Enough!

I often receive this question from my nonprofit clients: *How often should we post on our social media accounts without annoying our supporters?* This question illustrates a fundamental misunderstanding of how social media works. Sure, I certainly don't want to hear from every organization, business, news outlet, and person that I follow several times per day. But the reality is—there is no way that I ever will.

For example, in 2016, an average of 4.75 billion pieces of content was shared daily on Facebook. In the midst of this always-on, hyperconnected world, you need to be sharing compelling, visual stories of your impact with your online communities regularly. DAILY even. To address the fear of "annoying our supporters with too much communication," in my experience you will NOT annoy and "turn off" your fans and followers if:

◆ You are posting things that your audience wants to see

◆ You post when you have something interesting and of value to share

◆ You are contributing to their lives

◆ You remember that all social media posts work best when they are timely and relevant

If you are doing it right, you will not be irritating. You will be embraced, enjoyed, and celebrated by your online community.

research on the country you are visiting. The same goes for any social media channel. Before using it, you need to find out the terms that are used, the time required to maintain an account, the technical expertise required, and the resources needed. All of these questions will help you decide if a particular social media channel that your audience frequents is the best fit for your nonprofit.

How Much Time Does Participation in Social Media Take?

I've noticed a disturbing trend in the nonprofit sector. It seems that all too often, uninformed nonprofit boards and well-meaning but not-tech-savvy executive directors simply tack on the words "social media management" to the development or marketing professional's job description. This usually happens after a heated board meeting where it is decided that the nonprofit should be "doing social media." Then, an already over-extended individual is suddenly charged with getting one thousand Facebook fans, five thousand Twitter followers, and ten thousand new email sign-ups, practically overnight.

This poor person may already be a volunteer or may be part-time, struggling to finish all the other assigned tasks required of them such as writing grants, communicating with donors, organizing events, and coordinating volunteers (just to name a few). Well, you think, after all, social media is free. It only takes five minutes per day. It's just playing around on Facebook and Twitter. Right? *Wrong*. This kind of thinking is moving the sector backward! Social media is "free" to the same extent that getting a puppy as a present is "free"!

Many nonprofits now have staff members, even entire departments, dedicated to fundraising and marketing. As such, they should know the time commitment that relationship building entails. Nonprofits should be bucking this trend of just adding the work of social media onto an already over-capacity marketing or development staffer. The work of storytelling and social media cannot and should not be the responsibility of one person—back to **Chapter Two!**

As we have discussed, the real work of successfully engaging on or "doing" social media is extensive and labor-intensive. Think of it like starting an exercise plan—the more time and effort exerted, the more dramatic the results achieved. The amount of time spent on each social media task is directly proportional to the number of social channels on which the nonprofit participates and the results it wants to achieve. Such tasks include strategy and planning, learning, analysis, formatting, listening, writing, responding, thanking, measurement, reporting, continuous improvement, and exploring.

For nonprofit boards and executives to believe that "doing social media" is simple, free, and painless, they need to be apprised of the complexity of such efforts and how these efforts can result in an increased base of support and "conversation" about the cause. As long as progress is slow and steady, resources should continue to be allocated to these efforts. Instant results cannot be expected or realistic.

How Do We Get More Fans and Followers?

I know a lot of nonprofit professionals and marketing professionals. They have two things in common. Both groups want to know the most surefire and the fastest way to grow their fans and followers on social media channels. To illustrate, here are three common questions I receive every week in my in-box and on my Twitter feed:

- ◆ "How can I get ten thousand fans on my Facebook page?"

- ◆ "My competitor has 2,500 followers on Twitter. How can I get that same number?"

- ◆ "No one is following me on Pinterest. I need more followers, now!"

These are certainly valid concerns. However, I think they are missing the point. If no one is listening, then you may need to reevaluate what you are doing. Using social media effectively is about building long-lasting relationships with your donors and supporters. When you do this, you can then find out what is most important to them and tailor your content (information and resources) to their interests, passions, and desires. This will lead to more engagement, discussion, sharing, and—guess what?—donations.

Being a go-to resource in your field should be the main goal of any social media strategy. If your organization is the authority on a topic, if you have credibility and people are listening to you, and if people are sharing your information with their own networks (and people don't do this lightly), then you are headed for success!

Getting the *right* fans and followers—aka potential donors and volunteers, the people who care, the people who will take action on your behalf—is the key to success on social media platforms. The right fans and followers do not equate to everyone with a pulse. Sure, there are services where you can

Julia's Nonprofit Social Media Checklist

❑ Is your content relevant to your audience? Does it pass the "will they care" test?

❑ Is your post, tweet, or photo meant to elicit engagement—likes, shares, or comments?

❑ Do you have social share buttons on your website, blog posts, and thank-you pages?

❑ Do you have links to your social media accounts on all online marketing materials?

❑ Do you understand the unique culture of each social network?

❑ Are you posting at the ideal time for your audience?

❑ Are you posting a good mix of links, photos, videos, and text?

❑ Do you frequently look for and share resources and content from outside sources (with attribution) that are relevant and exciting to your audience?

❑ Do you thank your community members when they share, comment, like, and retweet?

❑ Are you strategically posting to become the go-to resource in your cause area?

❑ Are you always looking for ways to connect with your supporters online?

❑ Do you create your own eye-catching graphics using free or low-cost tools like Canva or PicMonkey?

❑ Do your supporters know you are active on social networks? Have you told them?

❑ Do you make it easy and compelling for your online community of fans and followers to spread the word about your cause?

❑ Are you collecting and sharing success stories and testimonials?

❑ Do you consistently demonstrate the impact of your work across social media channels?

❑ Are you listening and responding to comments and questions on your blog and social media platforms?

❑ Do you post to one social network at least once per day?

purchase fans and followers but what value does that provide? Most of these accounts are spambots who will never donate or visit your website.

Instead, focus your energies on the donors and supporters that you *do* have. They are your best brand ambassadors! How can they be acknowledged, groomed, and cultivated to spread the word? Word-of-mouth marketing is the best kind of marketing after all!

How Do We Get Our Fans and Followers to Share Our Posts and Tweets?

Getting your online community to share your content is the gold standard of social media. Likes and comments are all well and good but getting someone to share your post, your blog, or your tweet is what exposes your message to a wider audience. When you receive a lot of shares, you are no longer just "preaching to the choir." You are reaching out to new people who may have an affinity for your cause and want to join the fold.

Sharing is the most powerful action that an individual may take on social media. It requires more investment than passively, scrolling, reading, or even clicking "like" on a post. So then comes the million-dollar question: How do we get more people to share our content? Getting people to share isn't a cake walk but it is doable, and many nonprofits are doing it very well.

There are several proven methods to get more social media shares. First, make your content about your audience members and what they want to see, hear, and read. Do you mostly share information that talks about how great you are? While sharing testimonials and success stories featuring the people that you have helped works great on social media, always promoting your organizational accomplishments is not.

People want to see their beliefs conveyed in the content they share on social networks. Remember the theme of knowing your target audience that we discussed in **Part One**? The same holds true here. Make sure you know your audience members and what they stand for. Your social media content should reflect the values of your online community members and help them see themselves within it.

Content that gets shared on social media is also eye-catching. That means video that plays automatically in the news feed or a colorful photo of people engaged in an activity. Think about how you consume media nowadays—with ten Google Chrome tabs open while texting and scrolling through Facebook on your phone, maybe with the TV on in the background. We are all distracted; this is not news. If your post doesn't catch my eye while I am perusing the latest photos of my friend's vacation or the latest tweets from my favorite celebrities, then you are out of luck.

To combat social media overload, post many different types of content (articles, photos, videos, and text) to see what works best for your audience. Bright, clear photos of people smiling at the camera or in action shots always work best because they catch the eye and resonate with most.

To get shares, the post needs to elicit some kind of reaction from the reader or viewer. In other words, it needs to be emotional. Nonprofits have a distinct advantage when sharing stories on social media. They often have stories that can make people angry, or sad, or happy. When was the last time your local insurance agent could get you to feel extreme passion like that? (Nothing against insurance agents. They do important work!)

Think about the emotion you felt when you first watched a viral video like Caine's Arcade, Kony 2012, Chewbacca Mom, or any of the most popular videos that you have seen online. Take notes on what is currently being shared widely online and how it makes you feel.

To get more shares, each story you share on social media should have some purpose, some reason to exist. It should spur people to action. It should make them so mad or so moved that they can't help but press the share button and tell everyone they know.

When sharing a post or retweeting a link on social media, people share what makes them look good. They share content to prove something to their friends—about their values, their views, and their personality. It really is as simple as that. Are they trying to be witty, funny, serious, academic, nerdy, hip, or ironic? Thinking in this way, when posting a piece of content on social media, ask yourself: *If I shared this with my personal social networks, how would it make me look in the eyes of my friends, coworkers, and family members?*

Other popular types of content that people share widely are predominantly funny, helpful, and/or useful. That's due to the way that people want to be perceived by their networks. As a result, boring and basic photos of your latest board retreat will not get shared by your Facebook fans (other than the ones that are board members themselves).

Sharing something humorous or entertaining is pretty straightforward and easy to do on social media. Creating and posting content that is helpful and useful is where a lot of nonprofits get tripped up.

Isn't Social Media Just for "Slacktivists"?

The word "slacktivist" has surfaced so much of late that I feel the need to write a defense of the controversial practice. "Slacktivism" can be loosely defined as the support of a cause via minimal effort on the part of the supporter such as sharing a social media post or signing an online petition. It takes no time at all for someone to be an "activist" in this sense.

UNICEF Sweden aims to shock and awe us into doing more than just clicking the like button. In a recent ad campaign, it featured a video of a poverty-stricken child in a dank, dirty room speaking these words: "[My] mom got sick . . . [b]ut I think everything will be alright. Today UNICEF Sweden has 177[,]000 likes on Facebook. Maybe they will reach 200[,]000 by summer. Then we should be alright." Then UNICEF Sweden blatantly adds: "Likes don't save lives. Money does." (Rather ironically, they posted this all over social media sites and created a video for YouTube.) The point of the UNICEF campaign is that people who may like it on Facebook probably won't end up being donors. (Whether or not UNICEF has actually researched this disconnect is not clear.)

I have worked with many nonprofit organizations on their social media strategies. They have dedicated hundreds if not thousands of hours to connecting with stakeholders, engaging community members, and educating the public about their social issue. I feel that UNICEF's attacks on so-called "slacktivists" (anyone who takes action online) are harmful to nonprofits. This notion of "slacktivism" perpetuates the unhelpful, unproductive, and antiquated notion held by nonprofits that allocating and spending resources on social media is a waste of time. In my opinion and in

Facebook Could Save Your Life

The American Red Cross always does a stellar job of sharing helpful information and resources with its online communities. During hurricane season, their Facebook page continually posts updates on preparing for storms and dealing with the aftermath. In the hot summer months, their social media accounts remind people to check in with elderly friends and relatives as well as helpful information for keeping pets out of danger and staying hydrated. This type of timely, relevant, and useful content gets shared widely among their fans and followers. Find them on Facebook at *facebook.com/redcross*.

 stories from the real world

the face of research and best practices on the subject, educating a fan base and engaging directly with stakeholders is *never* a waste of time.

Effective fundraising is about telling a story and showing donors the impact their contribution will have on a cause about which they care passionately. It's about evoking positive emotions—saving children, protecting the environment, building a school—not about creating a shame spiral where your supporters are made to feel terrible. Rather than fighting the alleged effect of "slacktivism," nonprofits should reexamine their fundraising, marketing, and social media programs altogether. And if UNICEF Sweden were really against this form of passive activism, why wouldn't it make a real statement and delete its Facebook page entirely? (I didn't think so.)

UNICEF Sweden is minimizing the reality that more and more charities are effectively using social media tools to raise awareness and money for their causes. Dispelling UNICEF Sweden's notion that people who take action online don't actually donate money to nonprofit causes, the American Red Cross found in a 2014 survey that personal appeals from friends (often using email and social media) were the most effective way to raise funds. It also found that its social media fans were a very generous group overall with more than 71 percent donating to a charity in the past year and 60 percent of those donors giving online.

Social media efforts cannot exist in a silo. Ideally, they should exist hand-in-hand with the marketing, fundraising, community services, human resources, and programmatic efforts of the entire organization. Therefore, social media failure cannot solely be blamed for lack of donations to your organization.

Do not get discouraged by the sheer amount of tools, platforms, and channels available to you. Social media is not a fad or a trend; it has completely revolutionized marketing, fundraising, even basic human interactions. The tools will undoubtedly evolve and change, but the principle of connecting with your donors and supporters where they are and giving them information that they want will not.

I have seen even the smallest nonprofits create vibrant, engaged communities using social media. The key is to stay focused on your goals while remaining creative, authentic, and accessible. Your donors, supporters, and stakeholders are all using social media to discuss the issues that they feel passionately about—so jump into the conversation and make some waves.

To Recap

◆ The keys to achieving your goals with social media lie in knowing your audience members well and creating content tailored specifically to their interests.

◆ The "three Ds"—Diversification of channels, Dedication to strategy, and Dynamic content through stories, visuals, and videos—will help ensure success on social media for your nonprofit.

◆ When choosing social media channels, nonprofits should consider their audience, their goals, and their staff capacity to manage it all.

◆ Nonprofits should use social media as an avenue to tell their stories and to provide an inside glimpse into their work and their impact.

Chapter Twelve

Visuals and Video—Spice Up Your Storytelling

IN THIS CHAPTER

- ····▸ The benefits of using visuals and video
- ····▸ Tools to create visuals on a shoestring
- ····▸ Ways to use video to tell your nonprofit's story, connect with donors, and raise awareness for your cause

There is no doubt that visuals and video rule the social web. The social media mantra of "Show, Don't Tell" can be heard loud and clear via the most successful viral content. According to a study by HubSpot, social media posts that include photos receive 53 percent more likes and garner 104 percent more comments than those without pictures. Facebook reported in 2015 that its users watch eight billion videos per day on the platform. The network has also indicated that Facebook Live videos will be given higher priority in the news feed over regular videos, as its users spend three times as long watching live videos. Snapchat claimed ten billion daily video views in 2016. YouTube remains the second biggest search engine in the world (owned by the largest one). All of these numbers continue to climb month after month as the popularity and proliferation of digital video gain even more traction.

Visuals and video are the best performing types of content across all social networks including Facebook, Twitter, and Instagram. If you are the manager of your nonprofit's marketing and fundraising communications, you have undoubtedly experienced this for yourself—visual content receives the most traction from your fans and followers, hands down. The reasons why are easy to understand. We live in a cluttered, noisy digital landscape full of colorful, loud, and vibrant imagery, all trying to capture a piece of our fractured attention. People are reading less on social media and watching more videos. They are consuming more information in a shorter time frame. Your donors and potential supporters want to see your work as it happens, they want to feel as if they are a direct part of the action, and they want visual confirmation that their donations are making an impact and a difference.

The question is not *if* your nonprofit should use visuals and video in your digital storytelling but *how*. Often, this is much easier said than done for many nonprofit organizations. What if you do not have a graphic design background or the money to hire a professional videographer? What if your nonprofit does not already have eye-catching photos and videos that showcase your clients and your work? The answer is that you just need to get creative. Creating great visuals and videos will not be easy and will not happen overnight, but your efforts will ensure that you increase your engagement on social networks, much more than only posting text.

This chapter will walk you through the basics of creating great visuals on a shoestring budget, ways to use video for more compelling digital storytelling, uses of long-form vs. short-form video, and places to incorporate visuals and video to form a deeper connection with your donors and potential supporters.

Creating Visuals on a Shoestring

One way to create visuals like photos and graphics to use in your digital storytelling without a huge budget is to do it yourself. Having a tiny budget is no longer an excuse for creating text-heavy stories free of visuals! You can edit images and create unique graphics yourself with easy-to-use, free or low-cost editing tools such as Canva, PicMonkey, PostCreator, Picktochart, and Pablo by Buffer as alternatives to Photoshop. The explosion of mobile photo editing and design apps like Instagram, Boomerang, Ripl, WordSwag, PicStitch, and Over allow anyone capturing images with a mobile phone to enhance those photos using filters, stickers, and text overlay. Sharing a photo of a volunteer and putting the volunteer's story in the caption below it is great, but adding a short quote in text on top of the photo can be even more impactful.

Photo collages are hugely popular on social media. Using your smartphone or tablet, download a collage app. PicStitch is my favorite, and it's free.

Creating a collage of photos adds a deeper element of interest and is an excellent way to incorporate multiple perspectives. Collages often break the monotony of the news feed on Facebook and garner a lot of engagement and likes.

The best part of creating your own images and graphics is that you do not have to worry about copyright infringement or running into any legal issues involving ownership of images. You can also add your logo and organization's branding to the graphics and photos to help spread awareness of your nonprofit even further.

So if you can't hire a professional photographer, grab that smartphone and take your own photos.

I frequently use mobile apps such as WordSwag to create quick and compelling visuals to accompany blog articles and social media posts.

Example

Snap a photo of your desk, the food pantry, the children's room (without people in it if you have confidentiality concerns), art created by clients, or a thank-you note sent your way. The little things that may seem insignificant often work very well on social media. The pictures do not have to be works of art! Amateur, honest, authentic photos that give insight into the everyday happenings of your organization will be well-received and can enhance the stories you are telling.

Keep in mind that people love to have a visual glimpse behind the scenes, especially as an event is unfolding. It makes them feel a deeper connection to you and to your organization. It also shows that your nonprofit is accessible and transparent, which only increases goodwill.

Nonprofits should also actively solicit user-generated visuals from among their supporters and online community members. Ever heard of the #IceBucketChallenge? Peter Frates (from my hometown of Beverly, Massachusetts) created the social media challenge using just a hashtag to raise awareness of the devastating effects of ALS. There was no budget and no marketing war chest. No celebrities had been signed up (in the very beginning). It was a simple idea that happened to catch on and take the social media world by storm.

I am not advising you to attempt to recreate the unprecedented success of the Ice Bucket Challenge. However, I think that creating a fun, easy-to-do challenge and encouraging your supporters to spread the word with a hashtag is an excellent method to collect their photos, videos, and stories. Yes, it will certainly take some work and elbow grease (and unfortunately, you may not get Eddie Vedder and Bill Gates to participate) but, in the end, you should have a variety of visuals from which to pull and use in your marketing and fundraising. (Be sure to note that photo and video permissions should be explicit when participating in a challenge like this.)

Using Video to Catalyze Social Media Storytelling

Video is an incredibly effective way to tell a story. For nonprofits, it is a critical way to raise even more funds. A Google study has found that 57 percent of people who watch a video made by a nonprofit then go on to make a donation. *Over half!!!* Here are several practical ways that nonprofits can use video to deepen their connection with current donors and to reach more potential supporters:

Tell Inspiring Stories

This book is focused on storytelling. When that is coupled with the potential of video, storytelling remains the most compelling and engaging type of content out there for nonprofits to achieve results consistent with their goals and SMART objectives. Nothing can compete online with a well-told story in video format. Nonprofits that do well in this space often share a mix of longer-form, professionally shot and edited videos and in-the-moment snapshot stories about their work in the field.

Look back to the storytelling calendar that you created in **Chapter Three** and your social media content calendar. Where would incorporating video make the most sense? Always be thinking like a news journalist in this way. Take into account all of the events and happenings in your organization and community and figure out ways to take and share great video clips that can augment the story.

An excellent example of a storytelling video comes from the Chronicle Season of Sharing Fund: "Meet Bobbie and Ia." In this video, we hear the inspiring story of Bobbie, a homeless woman who was helped by the Chronicle Season of Sharing Fund to become more empowered and more hopeful. Viewers also meet Ia, a person who does not have a lot of money but still gives, and she tells you why. I get chills watching this simple video. Watch its videos at *youtube. com/user/seasonofsharing.*

Bring People "Into the Kitchen"

Once, when I went out to a very nice dinner with my husband, the owner of the restaurant came over to our table and asked us how we liked the food. After we had raved about it for about ten minutes, he offered to take us to the kitchen and meet the chef. We met the chef, got a brief tour of the kitchen, saw how things actually worked, and were even more blown away. Needless to say, we are now lifelong customers of that particular restaurant.

How can you bring people into your "kitchen" using video? How can you make them feel special and more connected to your organization? The answer: Showcase your organization's personality by posting brief, behind-the-scenes videos of your organization at work. An example of this is an Instagram video from UNICEF where staff is assembling the Trick or Treat

---

Consider the Channel

After you have recorded your video, be sure to upload the video directly to each individual social media platform. This is a more effective tactic than posting a link to the video! When you upload a video and share it directly to Facebook, Twitter, and Instagram, your video will automatically start playing when it comes up in the news feed or update stream.

Because videos play automatically in this way but play silently until the viewer clicks on them, you need to grab people's attention in that first frame. Think about what you can do to entice people to click on the sound button and watch the full video. Need some ideas for fantastic nonprofit videos that catch the eye and make you watch until the end? Check out the DoGooder Awards on YouTube at *youtube.com/user/ nonprofitvideoawards.* CauseVox also has a fabulous free Starter Guide to Nonprofit Video Storytelling at *causevox.com.*

practical
tip

for UNICEF boxes. This video has the added bonus of asking us to "stay tuned" to find out who its celebrity ambassador will be at the event. Watch UNICEF's videos at *instagram.com/unicefusa*.

Representative Eric Swalwell (D-Ca.) wanted to make a big impression when he voted against a controversial bill making it harder for women to have abortions, so he recorded his vote in a video and posted it on Vine. This short video raised awareness about the cause, the congressman, and the issue at hand. It also demonstrated to his constituents that he was active and involved around a critical issue. Watch Congressman Swalwell's videos on Vine under the account *RepSwalwell.*

Nonprofits of all sizes can post videos of the small things they do every day like answering the phone, planting a tree, giving away toys, or helping with homework. Events happening right outside the office doors or in the community are also fodder for short, in-the-moment videos. Human Rights Campaign (HRC) used Vine to highlight an anti-LGBT protest going on in front of its building as it happened. Watch HRC's videos on Vine under the account *HRC.*

Another great behind-the-scenes video was created by National Geographic to give a glimpse into the items that go into one of its photographer's camera bags. Watch National Geographic Society's videos at *instagram.com/natgeo.*

Show Donors the Love

Your donors made the decision to give money to your organization. This imparts a responsibility on your nonprofit to use the money wisely and responsibly and to communicate the results you achieve with them. Storytelling with video provides an intimate way to communicate the results that donors' gifts helped produce and shows potential donors and supporters that your organization is a good steward of funds.

Heal the Bay California has helped pass statewide legislation to protect the environment and the oceans. Its Instagram account frequently posts action videos and gorgeous landscape shots where it lets the beautiful ocean and surf at the Venice Beach Pier (places it actively helps to clean and preserve) do the talking. See its photos and videos at *instagram.com/healthebay.*

Showcasing real stories from real people who have benefited from your work in a video is sure to get people excited. The organization, charity: water, regularly posts interesting, unique videos featuring the people and the villagers whose lives have been changed by clean water. Watch its videos on its website at *charitywater.org* or at its Instagram account on *instagram.com/charitywater*.

Along with showcasing impact, video can be a more personal way to acknowledge and thank donors and supporters, either for donating to a particular campaign, helping the nonprofit reach a fundraising goal, attending an event, or even just following you on Facebook.

To Go With a Pro or Not?

There are two main categories of nonprofit video: amateur and professional.

Professional videos tend to be longer in length and formally staged and shot. These videos involve a lot of preparation and are created by a professional videographer or filmmaking studio, usually incorporating smooth edits, transitions, voice-overs, music, and more. Professional, longer-form videos are best used at gala fundraising events, on your YouTube channel, in your major gift solicitation materials (on a DVD), and on the donate page of your website.

Amateur videos are ones created by staff, volunteers, clients, and other stakeholders—people without formal experience or training. These videos work best on social media channels where short (thirty seconds or less), spontaneous videos rule.

With the proliferation of smartphones, tablets, and handheld video cameras (like the GoPro), along with microvideo apps such as Snapchat, Vine, Instagram, and Dubsmash, we all have the capability to be mini filmmakers. No matter your budget, your staff capacity, or your technical knowledge, there is no excuse for your nonprofit not to be sharing stories via video.

I can't tell you definitively which type of video will work best for your particular fundraising and marketing goals, your budget, and your audience. I *can* tell you that in my experience, on social media, people will not watch a long, five-minute video on the history of your organization. They often will not even watch a thirty-second video all the way through! In the digital space, people gravitate toward authentic, emotional stories from real people in a shorter, more informal format. The best strategy is to incorporate some long-form video with your short, in-the-moment video content for maximum success.

food for thought

Children's Hospital Colorado Foundation shared a fantastic video called, "Thank You for Supporting Kids Like Me," on YouTube, featuring several children who have received treatment there. The children express their sincere thanks to the doctors, staff, and people who give to the hospital. I dare you to watch with a dry eye! Watch its videos on YouTube at *youtube.com/user/TCHFoundation.*

How to Use Live-Streaming Video to Share Stories as They Happen

What do we mean by "live-streaming video"? This means filming a video live and broadcasting it via social media. It may sound terrifying to the uninitiated but take note: Live-streaming video is becoming the most popular form of video content on the web today. With nonprofits across the sector continuously being accused of shying away from the spotlight and spending all of their money on administrative costs, I see live-streaming video as an innovative way to get out of the shadows, become more transparent, and create an authentic connection with supporters—all things that nonprofits and donors alike are craving!

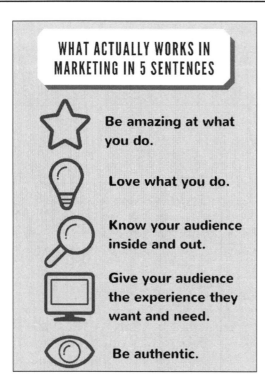

WHAT ACTUALLY WORKS IN MARKETING IN 5 SENTENCES

Be amazing at what you do.

Love what you do.

Know your audience inside and out.

Give your audience the experience they want and need.

Be authentic.

I frequently use mobile apps such as WordSwag to create quick and colorful visuals (see image) to accompany blog articles and social media posts.

Example

Live-streaming videos are broadcast almost exclusively through mobile apps like Facebook Live, Blab, Periscope, or Google Hangout. The tool that you use is not important as long as you do some research into what your audience members are using and which platforms they prefer. The videos are then stored within the platform for later viewing. They can also be downloaded and used again, if you so choose, on your nonprofit website or blog, for example. If your goal is to cultivate deeper relationships with your supporters and to get more exposure for your cause, live-streaming video may be a tactic to consider.

In this section, I will share some ideas of how nonprofits can use live-streaming video to connect with their audience and tell their stories, all with the added benefit of increased reach on social media platforms.

Conduct Live Interviews

The Metropolitan Museum of Art enlisted Brinda Kumar, a researcher and curator of the "Nasreen Mohamedi" exhibition, to walk viewers in real time through the exhibition with Sree Sreenivasan, The Met's Chief Digital Officer. This real-time interaction with people who work at the Met serves to break down walls and encourages people to ask questions, driving engagement and raising awareness of its latest exhibition. Watch its videos at *facebook.com/metmuseum/videos*.

Committed to transparency and accessibility in philanthropy, Bill & Melinda Gates Foundation CEO, Sue Desmond-Hellmann, often takes questions and comments from viewers live on Facebook. Viewers can ask questions about currently funded projects, planned activities, and trends in the sector as well as express their opinions on the topic at hand. Watch its videos at *facebook.com/gatesfoundation/videos*.

Go Live from the Field

What could be better fodder for a live-streaming broadcast than a dive off the coast of California? Nonprofit *explore.org* followed oceanographer Sylvia A. Earle as she explored the Channel Islands' kelp forest. Knowing its Facebook fans are passionate about conserving the kelp forests and the aquatic creatures who live there, the video provides a live, in-the-moment glimpse into its work and the beautiful environment it is preserving. Watch its videos at *facebook.com/endangeredanimals/videos*.

The Humane Society of the United States uses live-streaming video to take supporters directly into the field of animal care and rescue. Through live streaming baby raccoon and baby bird feedings, it invites its supporters and anyone interested in animals to ask questions of wildlife experts and interact with staff and volunteers. Watch its videos at *facebook.com/humanesociety/videos*.

Take Viewers Live Backstage

Disease research and advocacy organization Fred Hutch (formerly the Fred Hutchinson Cancer Research Center) invites viewers "into the kitchen" to talk with a featured chef at its big fundraiser, the Premier Chefs Dinner. This not only creates buzz for the event but it also helps raise money from people who are unable to physically attend the fundraiser. Watch its videos at *facebook.com/HutchinsonCenter/videos*.

Organized to leverage the power of celebrities to raise money for children living in poverty, Red Nose Day USA featured a live, backstage conversation among actresses, Jane Lynch, Yvette Nicole Brown, and Mayim Bialik. The broadcast helped raise awareness of Red Nose Day USA as well as raise money for the organization. Watch its videos at *facebook.com/RedNoseDayUSA/videos*.

Broadcast Live from an Event

The New York Public Library (NYPL) hosted a special story time in front of City Hall to raise awareness about its early literacy programs and to advocate for more investment in libraries. In the captions of the live video, available for viewing afterward, the NYPL encouraged people to take action on behalf of library funding and provided direct links to places where viewers could get more information and get involved. Watch its videos at *facebook.com/nypl/videos*.

Live streaming doesn't have to capture dramatic moments, but when it does it's very effective for mobilizing supporters—for example, when Greenpeace USA Executive Director, Annie Leonard, was interviewed live in front of the US Capitol, moments after being arrested at a #democracyawakens protest. Watch its videos at *facebook.com/greenpeaceusa/videos*.

Host a Live Q&A or AMA (Ask Me Anything)

This type of interactive event can be a live, exclusive, invite-only Google Hangout with the executive director and board chair, a public event such as a TweetChat on Twitter, or a live-streaming video interview on Facebook. Live Q&As require minimal planning (just make sure all the technology is working beforehand) and have the added benefit of providing you with a lot of content afterward that you can then re-use on your website, your email newsletter, and your blog.

Invite supporters and those curious about your cause to a live AMA with the executive director, key staff person, major donor, or, better yet, a person that has directly benefited from your programs and services. This type of live video can be very lively and usually generates a lot of great questions and comments.

The possibilities of and ways to use live-streaming video to tell your story are only as limited as your creativity. Here are four more ideas for live broadcasts that will definitely engage fans and get more supporters on board:

- ◆ *Live video series.* Consider creating an entire series that broadcasts at the same time and day each week—much like a TV show or a TweetChat—so that your fans can count on it and put it on their calendars. Viewership will need to build over time, but your supporters will come to rely on this broadcast as a means of learning about the latest news at your organization and the most current results of your work.

- ◆ *Newsjacking.* Comment on news and trending topics at the moment that people are talking about them. This is especially vital if you are an organization that mobilizes supporters and advocates on behalf of a particular issue and you want to go beyond sending text updates as legislation unfolds. If you are not able to express an opinion on behalf of your organization, simply ask your viewers what they think and what they would do.

- ◆ *Crowdsourcing.* Get live feedback on a question or solutions to a problem you are having. Openly share the process by which your organization makes decisions and let your donors and supporters contribute to the conversation. What better way to build ownership and camaraderie than a live, unfiltered discussion about a potential strategic decision of the organization?

- ◆ *Tell stories as they happen.* Once you get more comfortable with Facebook Live and the way it works and once you get a sense of how your audience will react, you can start telling the stories of the people, families, animals, and communities that you serve in real time. It may sound scary, but it can be exciting to share your work with the world as it happens.

Best Practices in Using Video on Social Media

Using video, live or otherwise, on social media platforms does require some knowledge of what works best. I would like to share several tips to help ensure that your videos get watched and shared by your fans and followers.

The most important tip in your video strategy for social media should be to keep it brief. Social networks are not the place to share your twenty-minute annual campaign video. YouTube found that you lose viewers of your videos in the first ten to twenty seconds. Keep your video down to no more than thirty seconds if you want it to be shared widely on social media channels.

Make sure to keep your video focused and on the subject. Much like your written storytelling, your video should ideally feature one story of a real person or family in a real situation. For example, instead of filming a thirty-minute video interviewing key staff members and volunteers, create a video series. As part of this video series, one video would be released per week featuring a short discussion with a different staff member or volunteer each time. Think back to the story series we discussed in **Chapter Six.** Do not try to tell all of your stories at once. No matter how compelling, they will get lost.

Ask Them What They Want

Before embarking on a live-streaming video series or investing a lot of time and money into developing an event to broadcast, take some time to discover what your audience wants.

Talk with your donors and those who are most passionate about your organization to determine the types of live-streaming online events in which they would be most likely to participate. Do they prefer live Q&As or interviews? Do they want to see more behind-the-scenes videos from the field? What would it take to get them to share the video on their own social networks? Getting your supporters, stakeholders, and donors involved in choosing the topics and format for your live-streaming videos is a surefire way to elicit goodwill and build loyalty.

food for thought

If you are posting a fundraising video where you are asking for donations, make the call to donate clear, explicit, and easy to carry out. Do not confuse video viewers and potential donors by stuffing in every possible request at the end of your video such as "Like us on Facebook!" or "Join our Mailing List!"

As always, bear in mind that videos which elicit an emotion work best and receive the most engagement on social media. If you create videos that elicit apathy, they will get ignored. Videos express situational context, body language, and sounds, making them so much more compelling than simple text. This is why a strong video is absolutely vital for your online audience to connect on an emotional level with your cause. Leverage the unique features of video to encourage further connection with your audience.

Facebook Video: Did You Know?

◆ "Native" videos (videos that are uploaded directly to Facebook as opposed to shared via a link) are the strongest performers in the news feed in terms of engagement (likes, comments, shares, and clicks).

◆ According to Facebook, 50 percent of Americans who use Facebook on a daily basis watch at least one video on the site every day.

◆ Facebook claims that its users drive eight billion video views per day on the platform.

For up-to-the-minute inspiration and guidance on creating great Facebook videos which will work across social media platforms, check out Facebook's website dedicated to providing tips for nonprofits at *nonprofits.fb.com*.

observation

As a busy nonprofit marketer and fundraiser, you know that time—yours, your donors, and your potential donors—is a precious resource not to be squandered. Thinking about all the moving parts involved in implementing a stellar video storytelling strategy may seem overwhelming at first. I will not sugarcoat the reality that creating and promoting great videos on social media is not easy.

However, I encourage all nonprofits, large and small, to embrace video storytelling as an exciting way to cultivate relationships with those who matter most to your organization. Video has taken over our social media streams and our mobile interactions in an unprecedented way. The younger generations have grown up with video everywhere and expect it on websites, on mobile apps, and especially on social media.

Nonprofits and causes need to leverage this technology and these online tools to their advantage. They have amazing, emotional stories to tell about their work and the people and communities that they serve every day. Nonprofits address complex problems to which an average person will often have difficulty relating, let alone thinking that they can make a difference or change a life. Video storytelling can help break down these barriers and increase understanding of the important work of the nonprofit sector as a whole.

Wouldn't you rather watch a compelling video from the local animal shelter or children's charity than an advertisement for a car or a brand of potato chips?

To Recap

◆ Visuals are required for all social media posts to get noticed, and they are a key ingredient in effective, engaging digital storytelling.

◆ There are many easy-to-use and low-cost tools available to nonprofits to accomplish video storytelling effectively themselves, whether it be creating great visuals, enhancing photos, or sharing and promoting videos.

◆ Shorter, more spontaneous, informal videos (thirty seconds or less) work best to drive engagement and action on social media channels.

◆ Get your donors and supporters involved in determining the topics and format of your organization's interactions with them. This will go a long way toward building interest and goodwill for your cause and mission.

◆ Some of the many ways for nonprofits to leverage the power of live-streaming video include hosting live Q&As, broadcasting behind the scenes from events, and showcasing work in the field as it happens.

Chapter Thirteen

Measuring Results and Building on Successes

IN THIS CHAPTER

···→ How to analyze the success of your storytelling efforts

···→ How to choose the metrics that matter

···→ How to use a measurement spreadsheet

···→ How to catalyze social media superfans

You may be tempted to skip this chapter. I would argue against that, as it is undoubtedly one of the most important chapters in this book. If you are not continually measuring your day-to-day activities against your goals, how will you know if all this blogging, posting, emailing, and tweeting has been successful? Without systematic and regular measurement and reporting, you may just keep spinning your wheels and wasting time pedaling fast but not actually get anywhere.

There are many reasons to collect data on your online storytelling activities. First, measuring your results will allow you to prove the worth of the work and justify the time and resources expended in achieving those results. Show those skeptics from **Chapter Seven** that telling stories is helping you achieve your nonprofit's goals and objectives. Prove to the board that the time and resources spent creating, collecting, and disseminating stories are raising awareness and funds for the organization. It may be slow going at first (in fact, it most certainly will be) but slow and steady wins the race, both in fables and in nonprofit marketing.

Second, if you never take the time to evaluate and analyze the results of your efforts, how will you know if it's working? And if you don't know if it's working, you will not know how to change your strategy based on what has been working and what hasn't been. Let's say that the months during which you publish four blog posts instead of three get a huge spike in website traffic and email sign-ups. You then know that pushing yourself to write one more blog post per month will improve your goal of getting more people to the website and encouraging more people to sign up to stay in touch with you.

Third, evaluation and analysis will result in less wasted time and money. If you have spent three months trying to figure out Pinterest but have not seen any movement toward your goals from it, then it's time to reevaluate what you are doing and work on improving your methods. Or it may be time to take a break from Pinterest and put more time into Twitter, where you are seeing a larger amount of engagement and activity. These are just a few examples of the ways that measurement of results can help you prioritize and allocate resources more effectively.

So why don't nonprofits take measurement more seriously? When reporting to funders about the effectiveness of programs and services, my bet is that your nonprofit is very organized in collecting and reporting data. Detailed outcomes measurement is hugely important to foundations these days, as any grant writer and development director knows! Unfortunately, many nonprofits do not feel that measuring and reporting are a very important part of digital marketing. They get so wrapped up in the day-to-day business of posting, blogging, and tweeting that they often never know if their efforts are bearing any fruit. This may stem from the fact that many nonprofits just do not know what to measure in their online efforts, or how. That's where I can help.

Common Metrics to Measure

Your measurement and data collection plan all depend on the goals and SMART objectives that you identified for your nonprofit in **Chapter Three.** Since the SMART objectives you came up with are very specific and measurable, they give you a clear path by which to collect the data and report on progress. Some other common metrics to measure when you carry out a storytelling campaign on social media are:

Number of Fans and Followers

These are also referred to as "vanity metrics." I briefly mentioned "vanity metrics" in **Chapter Three** because so many people get very hung up on them. It *is* important to make sure that the size and scope of your communities are growing and not decreasing. However, if you are not getting these fans and followers to do anything on behalf of your organization, then what good are large numbers? Businesses and celebrities often purchase thousands of Facebook fans and Twitter followers to make themselves look and feel good. Purchasing fans and followers is an incredibly damaging practice because those are fake accounts, representing people that will never engage with you and only exist to bring your social engagement numbers down.

Engagement

Engagement is a much more reliable measure of your efforts. Are your fans and followers liking, commenting, and clicking on your posts? When you post a photo, video, or link, does anyone respond? Or are there crickets? Engagement metrics are useful in figuring out what your community values and what types of stories resonate.

Share Counts

You are sharing stories and helpful resources on social media, on your blog, and through your email newsletter. Are your online community members responding by sharing them even further with their social networks? Getting a share, retweet, reblog, repin, and the like is the elusive gold standard for your social media and storytelling efforts.

Sentiment

Sentiment refers to the general feeling that people have about your organization online. Is it positive? Negative? There are many tools available that measure sentiment and overall "buzz" about the organization but you can also get information on this by conducting basic searches on Facebook and Twitter. Using a tool like Social Mention will give you in-depth analysis and even keywords used when people mention you online.

Attitude Change

This is much harder to measure, but if changing behaviors or social attitudes is part of your mission, you will need to take this into account. The evidence may be anecdotal at first, but hard data should follow. For example, the HRC championed the movement to legalize same-sex marriage. When the Supreme Court ruled that state-level bans on same-sex marriage were unconstitutional, thereby legalizing it nationally, the Internet responded in a hugely positive way. Major corporations like IBM,

Nike, and even JP Morgan all changed their Facebook profile photos to rainbows and wrote posts in support of the decision. It was fairly easy to see that mainstream public opinion in the United States had definitely changed to support same-sex marriage and the HRC should feel confident in taking some credit for that.

Interest in Your Website

To measure general interest in your website, you can use the free resource Google Analytics to measure the following attributes. Please note that Google Analytics frequently updates and changes the terms that they use to measure traffic, visitors, and referrals to the site. As of this writing, I recommend taking note of the following metrics available in your Google Analytics dashboard:

◆ *New and returning visitors.* The number and percentage of new and returning visitors that your website received over a given period of time (that you can define).

◆ *Bounce rate.* How many visitors left your site after only visiting one page?

◆ *Average session duration.* How much time did the average visitor spend on your site?

◆ *Behavior/site content.* Which pages did people frequent the most?

◆ *Acquisition.* How did people reach your site? Via social media or web search? What words did they search on to find your website?

Other metrics you want to consider are the number of readers of your blog, the number of blog comments, the most popular blog content in a certain time period, and the number of email subscribes and unsubscribes after each email campaign. A measurement spreadsheet template for use in tracking these metrics can be located in **Appendix D.**

What To Do with the Data

Remember that the numbers themselves will not tell you what you need to know to make improvements, tweak tactics, or change course. You will need to translate your data into something upon which you can act. Data is useful in that it can help you improve your methods. If you are not measuring what you are doing, how will you know that you are successful? Or that you are not successful? And what strategies work or don't work in achieving your goals and objectives?

Let's say that you discover that your Facebook posts with photos get much more engagement than your posts of articles or resources. What will you do with that information? Hopefully, you will use it to thoughtfully increase the number of photos that you post, thereby giving your audience what they implicitly want, and getting your organization even more engagement in the process.

Collecting and analyzing the data can help you gain more confidence in the direction of your social media efforts as well as demonstrate your successes, which will result in increased buy-in from supervisors and colleagues. Do you sometimes feel like you are spinning your wheels when using social media and digital tools? Thorough measurement and data analysis of your work can show you that you are in fact making a difference—or the data can

The What and Why of Google Analytics

Google Analytics is a free resource designed by Google to track the effectiveness of your website and your digital marketing efforts. The key is to set it up correctly so that you are accurately measuring and reporting on your nonprofit's specific online marketing goals.

Set it up in three easy steps:

1. Sign up for your free account at *bit.ly/SignUpGA.*

2. Follow the instructions to add the Google Analytics tracking code to your website pages. In just a few hours, you should be able to see your website data.

3. If you have specific metrics you want to measure in real time such as during a special event or a fundraising campaign, you can set up a customer alert. For example, if your website has more than a thousand visitors per day or if your donation page is getting more visits than usual.

confirm your fears. Either way, you don't want to send another tweet without knowing how it impacts your marketing and fundraising goals.

At the end of the day, donors want to support programs and services that work. If you are reaching more clients via social media channels, let your donors know! If you organize a hashtag campaign that generates a lot of engagement and sharing, then let your supporters know that they are involved in this success. People like to be a part of a winning team. Show them that they are helping you build a community and raising awareness of the issue that matters to them.

If your data show that more and more people are coming to your website, signing up for your email list, and attending your events, all due to your social media plan, then you should be able to get more resources behind it. This information should be able to energize the storytelling and social

---

Does Your Website Traffic = Donations?

Ask deeper questions and go beyond simple website traffic numbers or Facebook likes. For example:

◆ If a thousand people visited your website this month and only four made donations, how can that be improved?

◆ How many visits to the online donation page do you need to result in a gift?

◆ What is a website visitor really worth?

◆ Which external sites drive the most referrals? (In other words, where is your website traffic really coming from?)

◆ Do the visitors from these channels tend to result in a donation?

The more you understand about your website visitors and their behavior when they are on your website, the more you will be able to improve your site to garner even more donations.

You better believe that large companies know the estimated worth of each website visitor and the exact ways to funnel them from prospects into paying customers. As a nonprofit professional, you should also understand this process by analyzing your website traffic and the trends that may lead to increased or decreased online donations.

By having a complete picture of the ways in which donors and other visitors interact with your website, you can then tweak the content based on what works and what doesn't. If you are sending dozens of people to the donation page, but they are not actually entering their credit card information and making a gift, your website analytics will tell you where they dropped off. This will then help you design a better, more effective process for them.

media committee to gather even more stories, and could even soften the hard hearts of the social media skeptics in your organization. Keeping up the momentum on social media requires staff and a budget to continue and expand on the success.

Storytelling with social media is not a skill that comes preprogrammed into nonprofit organizations. Nonprofit professionals are often program-minded social workers, teachers, doctors, and community organizers. They are not marketing experts with MBAs in branding and digital media. Using the data you collect on the stories that you tell can impact the entire organization by changing the culture to one of transparency and openness. It can change hearts and minds and help dispel the myths and misconceptions about social media for nonprofits.

Extend the Life of Your Stories with Social Media Superfans

Throughout this book, you have learned how to create a culture of storytelling at your organization, collect and tell great stories, and use social media and online channels to disseminate these stories to a broad audience.

Storytelling and social media are not items that you can check off a to-do list. They are communication strategies and skills that must be honed every day if they are to bear fruit. One way to extend the life of the stories that you tell and keep up the momentum you have created is by keeping an eye out for your nonprofit's social media superfans.

Your social media superfans are those people who will share your stories far and wide and keep the ball rolling and the momentum building even while you are not at your desk! They are the superstars who like, comment, and share your Facebook posts, heart your Instagram photos, and retweet your tweets. They comment on the blog, share your emails, and always offer to share news and resources with their own social networks.

There are several things to consider when building your own cadre of social media superfans. You should not recruit them by the sheer number of followers alone. For example, a dedicated supporter of yours doesn't have to have fifteen thousand Twitter followers or four thousand Facebook friends to have influence over a significant number of people. They may be incredibly influential in a small niche that you want to engage.

It is important to recognize that just because someone is influential does not mean that your cause will resonate with them. Think about how

Ways to Use Social Media Superfans

The Massachusetts Conference for Women is an annual gathering of thousands of business people and entrepreneurs held in Boston. This prestigious conference has featured talks by high-powered, influential woman leaders like Kerry Washington, Arianna Huffington, and Hillary Clinton.

Each year, the conference committee invites social media enthusiasts to apply for their social media street team. Being selected for the street team means a free pass to the conference, which can cost upward of $185.

When selected, street team members receive weekly emails with prewritten tweets, Facebook and LinkedIn posts, Pinterest pins, and Instagram-ready photos and graphics. Everything is fully edited for character length and content and ready to cut and paste or upload onto the street team's individual social media accounts.

 **stories from the real world**

you cultivate major donors. A strategy that includes randomly contacting all the rich people in town even if they have never expressed an interest in your cause is faulty and will get you blacklisted. Be strategic in whom you contact to promote your nonprofit online and make sure it's an appropriate fit.

Qualities of Social Media Superfans

Let's look more closely at the qualities of social media superfans:

Engagement

Simply "liking" your Facebook page or following your organization on Twitter does not a superfan make. A superfan participates in the conversations you create and completes the actions and tasks you request. This can include sharing a post, signing a petition, and spreading the word about a cause.

Advocacy

A superfan will have your back during good times and bad. If there are naysayers or critics on your Facebook page or blog, a superfan will be there to respond and to defend you.

Evangelism

The most important aspect of superfans is their ability to personalize the information you share and get others involved in the cause. They believe so strongly in what you do that they are willing to go out on a limb and try to convince their friends and family to join the movement. This is the most powerful characteristic of superfans. Keep your eye out for these evangelists and make sure you are always thanking and rewarding them!

Don't forget to consistently acknowledge your social media superfans! Thank them profusely, offer them special access to your nonprofit, and show them the results of their efforts. They might only have forty-five LinkedIn connections, but their passion and interest are authentic and real—and often contagious.

Always be cultivating your current online advocates and thoughtfully create others. What the sector needs most is to actively develop and train the new generation of advocates for giving, standing up, and getting involved.

To get more superfans, actively look everywhere for people who are passionate about your cause. Don't ask them for their bank statement or their Twitter follower count. Engage them where they are.

Also, see what you can do to find your offline community and entice them to join you online. Use your events, support groups, community gatherings, lectures, seminars, and educational tours to encourage the people who support you offline to join you in your online communities. And vice versa!

A social media "superfans" online toolkit with examples from nonprofit organizations is included in **Appendix E.**

Did Your Storytelling and Social Media Plan Succeed?

Only you and your nonprofit constituents can determine if you have found success with your efforts in storytelling and social media. You may have found unexpected success in the form of the recruitment of a new board member, the development of a strategic community partnership, or the support of a local politician. Hopefully, you will also have found the success you were looking for in the form of increased revenue and inquiries, name recognition, support, affinity, and trust.

When looking the data you have collected, it is important to see trends over time, no matter how small. Are the numbers consistently growing? If you are following your plan and staying consistent and true to what you set out to do, great things can only follow.

I believe that, in analyzing your successes, you also need to evaluate your overall plan as well as its internal goals and objectives. When evaluating your efforts, make sure to ask these questions:

◆ Did we follow the plan for this marketing strategy? If not, why not?

◆ Did we stay on budget? If not, why not?

◆ What challenges (such as time, resources, money, management) did we encounter as part of this strategy?

◆ How did we overcome these challenges? (Be specific.)

◆ What feedback did we get from our target audience as a result of our efforts?

◆ Knowing what we know now, what should we have done differently?

◆ Should we use this strategy as a model for future efforts?

The two major ways you can tell that your stories are successful are if they inspired people to take action and if they inspired people to share them. Authenticity is key, as people can always smell a phony. Aim for authenticity in all of your communications but in social media especially, as it is the value so often lost there. Be true to your organization's values and ethics

---

See the Forest for the Trees

When measuring longer-term, big-picture results, ask the following:

Do you believe or can you prove even in some small way that you are helping to inspire social change? Are your blog posts, videos, and email news blasts inciting change in how people act or think? Are you provoking discussions, debate, and conversation on the issue?

Look at your organization's operations. Have requests for community presentations risen? Have caseloads increased or decreased? Do you have qualitative or anecdotal evidence of donor and supporter behavior and attitude changes as a direct result of your work?

At the end of the day, the impact on your overall organization's operations is what's necessary to further your work and increase your impact. Make sure these results do not get lost in a rush to count Facebook likes and Twitter retweets.

principle

and be supporter-centric in your communications. Remember that your organization itself isn't important, its *impact* is.

To get more people on board with your storytelling and social media efforts, be helpful and be credible. Aim to be a reliable source of information and a go-to resource in your field. Always be improving, learning, and exploring new ways of doing things.

Storytelling should not be used to exploit people's emotions only to collect donations. Great stories inspire staff and volunteers. They motivate loyal donors and entice new people to come into the fold.

Remember that *everyone* has a story. It might not be one that you can use right now, but it might lead you to an idea or a person who can help. Your nonprofit has stories to tell. Your donors and supporters want to hear these stories, and they want to share them. Give them the opportunity to do so, and reap the rewards.

To Recap

- ◆ Measurement is essential for determining if your storytelling and social media efforts have been successful or not and why. Do not discount its usefulness in your marketing and storytelling efforts.

- ◆ Sharing hard data and statistics isn't enough. You must know what story you want to tell with the data you have.

- ◆ Sample metrics to include in your measurement spreadsheet include engagement, website interest, and actions taken (based on your goals and SMART objectives).

- ◆ Social media superfans exist for your organization and should be cultivated and acknowledged frequently.

Appendix A – Storytelling Calendar

[Next Page]

Date	Event	Story to Tell	Person Responsible	Story to Collect	Person Responsible	Notes
May 15	Fundraising gala	Client impact story	Tom	Stories from donors who support us	Gayle	Make sure to take video!
July 9	Networking event fundraiser	Board member story	Tom	Stories from people at the event who have supported us	Tom	See if you can take video, include photos
August 17	Volunteer Orientation	Client impact story	Bonnie	None	N/A	Maybe include a story of a volunteer and what they gained

Appendix B – Social Media Content Calendar Template

[Next Page]

WEEK: July 22 Channel	Monday	Tuesday	Wednesday	Thursday - BIG FUNDRAISING EVENT	Friday
Facebook Page - Morning Post	Photo from the event over the weekend	Testimonial and video	Post about fundraising event tomorrow with fun video	#TBT (Throwback Thursday) - Fun photo	Photos from last night's event
Facebook Page - Afternoon Post	Reminder to register for Thursday's event	Link to blog post	Post 3 reasons to attend the event tomorrow with fun photo	Link to blog post promoting the event	Top Fundraisers, photo
Twitter - Morning Tweet	Tweet a photo from the event over the weekend	Retweet	Tweet about fundraising event tomorrow with fun video	#TBT (Throwback Thursday) - Fun photo	Photos from last night's event
Twitter - Afternoon Tweet	Retweet	#CharityTuesday - highlight a nonprofit partner	Tweet 3 reasons to attend the event tomorrow with fun photo	#ThankfulThursday - walk sponsor, photo	Top Fundraisers, photo
Twitter - Evening Tweet	Reminder to register for Thursday's event	Tweet out the blog post link	Reminder to register for Thursday's event	Tweet out the blog post link	TGIF, what's everyone doing this weekend

LinkedIn Profile	Reminder to register for Thursday's event	Link to blog post	Post about fundraising event tomorrow with link to registration	Link to blog post	Thank you for attending the event/thanks to our sponsors
LinkedIn Company Page	Reminder to register for Thursday's event	Link to blog post	Post about fundraising event tomorrow with link to registration	Link to blog post	Thank you for attending the event/thanks to our sponsors
Pinterest	Pin an infographic	Pin a neat "How To" post	Pin a photo from behind the scenes at the event	Pin a #TRT photo	Pin a fun quote/fun photo
Instagram	Post a picture of the office shot at a cool angle	Post a video of volunteer training	Share a photo from setting up the event	Post a photo of the event	Post a photo of the event
Blog	N/A	Top 10 Nutrition Tips	N/A	Post promoting the event - top 10 reasons to attend	N/A
Email Newsletter	N/A	N/A	Send email reminder about event tomorrow	N/A	N/A

Appendix C – Blog Editorial Calendar Template

[Next Page]

Day	Date	Objective	Content Bucket	Content Details	Post Title	Visual(s)	Notes
Monday	July 1	To get people to click on the blog post	Impact Story	Interview with client Susan and her daughter	How a Single Mother Beat Addiction	Photo of Susan at work	Get photo permission
Saturday	July 9	To get people to donate to the annual fund	Fundraising	Compelling story of another family	TBD	Video	Choose video to use

Appendix D – Measurement Spreadsheet Template

[Next Page]

	August	September	October	November	December	January	February
Overall Website (You can get this from Google Analytics)							
Users (Unique)							
Pageviews							
Average time on site							
Bounce rate (% who view only one page)							
Highest traffic single day							
Keywords (what they use to find you)							
Notes							
Website Content (page views)							
Most popular site content for the month							
Number of views of most popular content							
Second most popular site content for the month							
Number of views of second most popular content							
Home page views							
Notes							

Social Referrals to Website (page views)

Facebook							
Twitter							
LinkedIn							
Pinterest							
Instagram							
YouTube							
Most popular other referral source							
Notes							

Facebook Insights

Number of fans at end of month							
% change							
Post with the highest reach							
Reach							
Post with the second highest reach							
Reach							
Highest engagement post							
Engagement rate							
Second highest engagement post							
Engagement rate							
Average engagement % (eyeball estimate)							

Facebook Ads performance						
Twitter Analytics						
# of twitter followers						
% change						
# mentions						
Retweets of me						
Most retweeted tweet						
From analytics. Twitter.com - Overall impressions						
Average daily impressions						
Engagement rate (average)						
Link clicks						
Favorites						
Replies						
Email Marketing						
	N/A	N/A				
Email open rate						
Email click-through rate						
Most popular link clicked on in email						
# subscribers						

Appendix E – Social Media "Superfans" Online Tool Kit Checklist

This Online Tool Kit should be housed on your website and accessible to anyone who wants to become a Social Media Superfan!

Sample language for the Online Tool Kit web page:

Want to join our team of Social Media Superfans? Want to help spread the word about our organization and our impact? Email us for more details, and feel free to use the resources provided on this page!

CHECKLIST

❑ Updated data and statistics on your mission

❑ Videos people can share

❑ Testimonials and success stories

❑ List of relevant hash tags to include in social media posts

❑ Approved photos for distribution (with your logo or watermark)

❑ Logos

❑ Blog post ideas and templates

❑ Graphics to use on social media

❑ Sample press release

❑ Sample outreach email

❑ FAQs

❑ Talking Points

- ❏ Social media tip sheet

- ❏ Sample tweets

- ❏ Sample Facebook posts

- ❏ Sample LinkedIn posts

- ❏ Graphics for Instagram and Pinterest

Social Media Superfans Digital Tools:

- ❏ *GaggleAmp*—Nonprofits are able to widely distribute their content and messages by creating a network of people (called a "Gaggle") that share, Tweet, and post company-created messages and content.

- ❏ *Zuberance*—Zuberance offers a platform for identifying "Advocate Armies" and turning them into passionate Superfans for your business or your cause.

- ❏ *Dropbox*—Post sample social media posts, graphics, photos to share, and language in Dropbox for Social Media Superfans to use. Of course, the ideal place to store these materials is on your website!

Social Media Superfan Online Tool Kit examples:

- ❏ Leukemia & Lymphoma Society Light the Night Walk Social Media Tool Kit: *http://www.lightthenight.org/what/social toolkit*

- ❏ #GivingTuesday Social Media Tool Kit: *http://www.givingtuesday.org/ toolkits*

- ❏ MercyCorps Fundraiser's Tool Kit: *http://www.mercycorps.org/fundraisers-toolkit*

Index

Did you know that CharityChannel Press is the fastest growing publisher of books for busy nonprofit professionals? Here are some of our most popular titles.

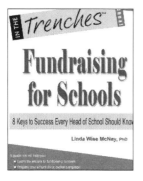
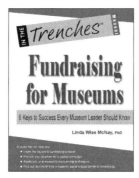

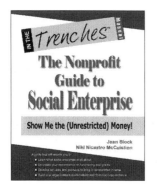

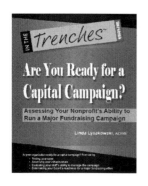
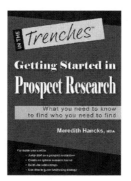

CharityChannel.com/bookstore

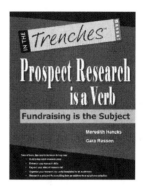

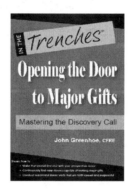

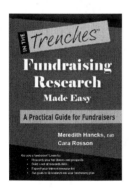

CharityChannel.com/bookstore

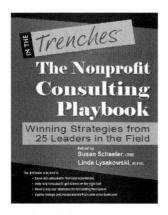
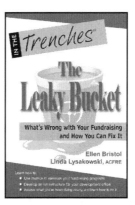
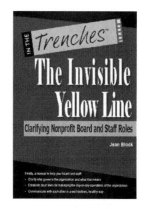

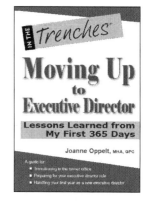

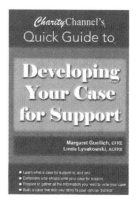

And more!

CharityChannel.com/bookstore

Made in the USA
San Bernardino, CA
13 June 2020